To Donald
I hope you enjoy!

KEEP ON PEDALING

Thanks

Keep on Pedaling

Jimmy Allen

KEEP ON PEDALING

Scripture taken from the New King James Version. Copyright © 1979, 1980, 1982 by Thomas Nelson, Inc. Used by permission. All rights reserved.

iUniverse books may be ordered through booksellers or by contacting:

iUniverse
1663 Liberty Drive
Bloomington, IN 47403
www.iuniverse.com
1-800-Authors (1-800-288-4677)

ISBN: 978-1-5320-1133-7 (sc)
ISBN: 978-1-5320-1132-0 (e)

Library of Congress Control Number: 2016921105

Print information available on the last page.

iUniverse rev. date: 01/06/2017

DEDICATION

This book is dedicated to all my friends and family. A big thanks, especially, to my wife June and our children: Jay and Lela Allen, Leslie and Jason Lairsey, Laurie and Steven Scarrow, and Amy Allen. Our grandchildren are the pot of gold at the end of the rainbow. Also, this book is for my sister Sonja and brother Mel.

Thanks to my friend Roy Rhodes for his
help in making the book a reality.

PROLOGUE

The journey to write this book started one night when I woke up and felt a stronger-than-ever urge to start recording some of my life experiences. I wanted my children and friends to know more about our family and about growing up in South Georgia.

I have never considered myself to be a writer, but the stories were real and alive in my head. Once I started writing, it was like seeing the memorable events come alive on paper.

Some stories are sad, some are funny, and I'm trying to make a point in others. I'll let you decide which are which. As I wrote this book, I wanted all who read it to feel as if they were in the places I tell about, with the same emotions that I had at the time.

Thank you so much for taking time to read this book. I truly hope you enjoy it.

Jimmy Allen

EDITOR'S NOTE

I first met Jimmy Allen and many of the friends he writes about in Homerville, Georgia sometime around the summer of 1964. He would have been fourteen, and I was thirteen. I was the outsider from Arkansas, come to stay a couple of weeks in Homerville each summer with my sister and her family, just for the fun of it.

What I quickly learned about Jimmy and his friends was that I wouldn't be considered an outsider for long. We were all fun-loving kids, growing up in small town America and blessed beyond all understanding, particularly with adults who cared about us and gave us the freedom to make a lot of stupid mistakes.

As you'll see in this book, Jimmy Allen is a big-hearted person. He was as a boy, and he remains so some fifty-plus years later. He is always thinking about other people and how to help them in the moment, but more than that, how to get them to see that life is good and should be lived to the fullest. That's help for a lifetime.

Jimmy first started sharing his stories on Facebook, and the response from his vast number of friends was immediate. They loved all these stories you're about to read. I watched their comments closely, fascinated by what they had to say about Jimmy's memories come alive in their minds.

I could tell that he was touching nerves and hearts with his recollections of growing up in South Georgia, a place he dearly loves. I imagined his friends looking up from their phones after reading a story, often laughing, sometimes brushing tears from their cheeks, always thinking, *That's the way it was. Life was sweet and sometimes it was bittersweet.*

And that's the effect that a great storyteller has on people.

I'm blessed to be part of this project. Thanks, Jimmy.

Roy Rhodes

What a Few of Jimmy's Facebook Friends Say About <u>Keep On Pedaling.</u>

If you keep writing humorous stories like that, based on true-life experiences with local characters you grew up with, you could become the next Lewis Grizzard!

Lanier Owen

I have really enjoyed your stories. I have often said I would like to write a book about being raised in Echols County and being the son of a Sheriff. Your stories encourage me to pursue that desire. You make it look easy. Keep them coming!

Lamar Raulerson

Love your stories so much...Takes me back.

Lynn Williams Wooldridge

Poignant story! I always look forward to your next tale! You never know what kind it will be.

Marty Dalton

I love your stories. They're full of wisdom.

Sally Humphries

Sweet story, Jimmy... I so enjoy reading your short stories.

Marilyn May Delprete

Your style of writing and formatting are so very pleasurable to read. It's like condensing the years into a couple of paragraphs.

Paul Barber

TABLE OF CONTENTS

Life in Echols and Clinch Counties

A South Georgia Boy's Life

My Sporting Life

My Working Life

Some Good People in My Life

Life is Good

Special Additions to My Life

KEEP ON PEDALING

I go through most of my days on the surface of life, not thinking very deeply about how best to live or what it all means. I believe most people are like me, thinking mostly about where we have to go today, what we need to do, who we want to see, and finally, what's for dinner.

But occasionally I catch myself going into some deeper thoughts about life. This first story is about both light and deep thinking.

One of my high school friends, John Barrett, and I decided one day to ride our bikes to Waycross, Georgia from Homerville, Georgia, a distance of about thirty miles by highway. Since we were in high school at the time, you could say our decision was a good example of light thinking. It was not a great idea. As my Mom later told me, we could have been run over, even killed. That's the reason I didn't tell her about our idea until after the fact.

We did make it to Waycross, and it took us several hours. We then started the return trip to Homerville. On the way back, we were close to the little town of Manor (pronounced Mainer) when some friends rode by in a truck, and we loaded our bikes up on the truck and went home. We rode a total of about fifty miles that afternoon, and, of course, we were on the old-fashioned one-speed bikes.

So here is the lighter thought. If you make a complete rotation on a bike pedal, you would go about one yard with the one rotation. So, how many rotations did it take for one bike to go the fifty miles we rode that day? The answer is 88,000 rotations, give or take some. WOW! That is a big number.

Now I will try to go a little deeper. In life, as with bike riding, we have to pedal one rotation at a time to get anywhere and to make life count for more than just getting up and going through a routine. At the same time, we have to try not to get run over.

I am a firm believer that the first rotation in life is to dream. We ought to have a vision of what we'd like to accomplish and how we could make the world a better place.

The second rotation is to plan and work our dreams into reality. We should always try to go forward. When we do fall or fail, which we will do often, there is a time to quit crying, get up, and start over.

The third rotation is to be encouragers and to accept encouragement in life.

The fourth rotation is to play the cards we are dealt. It's more fun to win with a losing hand than to win with a winning hand. Even worse is to lose with a winning hand.

One more important rotation: "If any of you lacks wisdom, let him ask of God, who gives to all liberally and without reproach, and it will be given to him." (James 1:5)

We need to make our rotations count before we pass another mile marker.

Life is good.

LIFE IN ECHOLS AND CLINCH COUNTIES

ECHOLS COUNTY

All my relatives were from Clinch and Echols counties. The two counties were next to each other in South Georgia. Both are on the Georgia and Florida state line, but Clinch extends slightly north of Echols. By knowing some things about these two counties, you will have a better understanding of my stories and where they take place. The largest town in Echols County is Statenville, which is about twenty miles away from Valdosta, the largest city in the area.

Echols was formed in 1858. The county was named after Brigadier General Robert Echols. He was a politician and died fighting in the Mexican War. Statenville, the county seat, was named after Captain James Staten who built the first store in the area.

When I was young, the county had a population of around two thousand people, and now is up to over four thousand. Out of 159 counties in Georgia, it is the least populated. Back when license plates were produced locally, all Echols county tags started with the numbers 159. I wish I could find one of those old tags.

As a youngster, I liked to brag that my Uncle Leon was the sheriff, Uncle Louis was the game warden, and Uncle J.H. was the state patrolman for the area. Our family had all the law officials on our side.

I found out that at one time Statenville was named Troublesome. I wish I knew more about how that name came about. Maybe they changed the name after my uncles made it into a good town.

I have heard tales, and I am certain they are true, that many years back, judges in places like Atlanta would sentence people to leave their cities, and they had to go to Echols county to live. When people in Echols County got in trouble, the judge there would sentence them to move out of the state, and they would go to Florida. I think Mexico is doing this to our country now.

Echols is an agricultural area with pine trees, honey, blueberries, and farm produce supplying most of the job base. Olive trees are now being planted and may be a future income supporter.

Echols County is a great place to live and to support a family.

GRANNY RAULERSON'S
HOME PLACE

Recently my head has been exploding with stories I should write, so here I go. My dad died when I was young. As I have gotten older, which has occurred much quicker than I ever thought it would, I realized I never got to hear my dad's stories about his youth, World War II, or his life in general. With that thought in mind, I will share some of my life's stories with you.

My starting point is when I was in the second grade. From time to time, my parents would separate, and my sister and I would find ourselves at my Grandmother Raulerson's home in Haylow, Georgia in Echols County.

Haylow was a turpentine community in those days, the late 1950s, and the town consisted of a small general store with a post office inside, the turpentine mill, and a few homes. The streets were dirt, and all the homes looked alike: wood framed, unpainted, and with small front and back porches. We visited with family and friends on the front porch and bathed in a wash pan with soap and a towel nearby on the back porch.

I saw my first movie in a tent in Haylow. It was a black-and-white cowboy movie, and the cost was a nickel. The people who owned the tent came through town once a year, set up for business for a week, and then moved on.

My grandmother's home didn't have electrical power or running water. On the positive side, she did have a wood-burning stove, screened-in windows and doors, an ice box, three outhouses, and a hand pump in the field behind the house.

Her cooking was great. I recall only two rules as a kid. One was to wait until the adults ate, and then it was the kids' turn. The second rule was to do what the adults told us to do. They were quick on the whip and short on words at my grandmother's home.

STORYTELLING

I really miss the family visits at my grandmother's home many years back. One Sunday each month, almost all of her children would show up for lunch and to visit on the front porch. She had eight adult children, four sons and four daughters plus lots of grandchildren. We kids would roam the town and woods, then eat lunch, and go to the porch to listen to the big talkers, my four uncles.

Louis, J.H., Sherman, and Leon Raulerson were great storytellers, and they competed to tell the best story of the day. Each of them was one-of-a-kind, but all of them had some common Raulerson traits. Those traits were stubbornness, belief in hard work, the importance of family time, the enjoyment of life, and the ability to laugh at themselves and at other people. If they ever told one of us kids to do something or if they warned us not to do something, it was for sure that we better do as they told us. They did not play the word game.

Strange, but I actually remember one story my Uncle J.H. told, and we are talking like fifty-five years ago when he told this yarn. I will try to share the best I can, and most likely, you will not be able to forget it either.

My Raulerson uncles were big deer hunters, and they all had twenty or more dogs. Each dog had a name and was his owner's pride and joy. Each brother thought his dogs were better than their brothers' dogs, so we always heard plenty of deer and dog stories.

Uncle J.H. said one time he put his dog out to run a deer, and it didn't come back that day. He said the dog just blasted through the swamp woods after the deer. Uncle J.H. checked back the next day, and the dog was not around. Of course, my other uncles were laughing at him for losing his best dog.

A day or so later, J.H. got a call and someone who knew him said they saw his dog running a deer near Lake City, Florida about forty miles south of Haylow. The next day my uncle got another call that the dog had been seen even farther south in Florida. During those days in South Georgia and north Florida, a lot of people knew my uncles and their dogs, since they were willing to take anyone hunting who wanted to go.

My other three uncles and the rest of us were in suspense listening to Uncle J.H.'s story.

Then, Uncle J.H. said he got a call that the dog was seen heading back to Georgia. About four days later, another caller reported that the dog was back in Georgia. My Uncle went back to where he let the dog out and as soon as he got there, he heard the dog barking and running, and he was right on the same deer.

Uncle J.H. got his gun and killed that big deer right there where he had let the dog out earlier that week. He said he loaded the deer up and took his dog home. Then he asked if any of his brothers needed any venison.

THE WAY IT WAS

First, I'll give you a few population facts about Haylow. In the mid-fifties the town had a total population of about 100 people, about half white and half black. All the jobs were related to the production of turpentine, pulpwood, or honey.

My dad worked in the woods as did my uncles, along with both white and black friends. I don't think we had much of a color barrier in Haylow. Men had to work and the ladies had plenty to do at home. Blacks and whites worked together in some of the hardest jobs ever. Color was no issue.

Housing for all was about the same. The only difference was that my uncles and some other of the whites had either a car or a truck.

When I stayed with my grandmother Raulerson in Haylow, my two playmates were James Rewis and Johnny Ray. We played and stayed in each other's homes and had many good times. I recall James getting a bike, the only one in town. He was quick to let Johnny and me ride it.

The bike didn't last long on those dirt roads, and it wasn't much fun to own the only bike in town. Johnny told me he loved going to my grandmother's house, she was so good to him, and he loved her cooking. James was white, and Johnny was black.

James ended up being one of the best beekeepers in South Georgia and is now retired. I had a conversation with Johnny many years back in Washington, D.C. We had a great time together at dinner, talking about the days. As we talked, he brought tears to my eyes. In fact, they're here now as I write this story. I recall how happy he was to see me that day. It was a great time for both of us.

This is the story that Johnny shared with me. I didn't know it until that day in Washington after we were grown up.

My uncle Leon, who was the Sheriff of Echols County, went to Johnny's house soon after he graduated from high school. Uncle Leon asked him what he was going to do with his life. There weren't many choices for Johnny as he didn't have the money for college and there weren't any good jobs in the area.

Shortly after that visit, Uncle Leon took Johnny to Jacksonville, Florida in the Sheriff's car and helped him enlist in the Navy. Then, a few weeks later, Leon carried Johnny back to Jacksonville for active duty. He encouraged him to do his best with this good opportunity and said he would help look after his family while he was gone.

That night in Washington, Johnny told me that when he was growing up in Haylow, my dad taught him how to drive a car and let him drive it around on his own. At that moment, tears were in both of our eyes. I thanked him for sharing that story with me.

Johnny said that my dad was the best man ever. He then added my grandmother, the Rewis family, Uncle Leon, and Uncle Lewis to the list.

While Johnny was in the military, he went to college and ended up getting a law degree, becoming a lawyer and an officer in the Navy. Now, he has his own law practice in Washington, D.C. He was elected to the city council there for many years and came very close to being the mayor.

Back in Echols County, they named the Echols County Library after him.

Yes, I'm proud of James, Johnny, Dad, and Uncle Leon.

We can make a difference in many lives by one kind action. Those people on the receiving end, such as Johnny, will never forget some very special people who helped him. I was happy to hear my Dad, Uncle Leon, and other relatives on his list of admired people.

THE BEAR HUNT

As I was going into the big ninth grade, Uncle Louis asked me if I wanted to help him with his beekeeping operation for about five weeks. The pay was three dollars per day with room and board at his house. Who could turn down an opportunity like that? Not me. That was big money for a boy in the 1960s, plus my Aunt Gladys was the best cook in South Georgia.

Breakfast, dinner, and supper, it was called at that time. Now, it's breakfast, lunch, and dinner. How did that change in terms ever happen? It took me years to learn when to show up at someone's home when they asked me to eat dinner with them.

I took the job. When I reported, Uncle Louis had purchased me a brand new pair of green rubber lace-up boots to work in. They were cool.

Aunt Gladys' typical meal was usually ready and waiting for us at noon, sharp. Every day, we had fresh peas, butter beans, snapped beans, creamed corn, fried chicken, roast and gravy with rice, cornbread, and boiled or fried okra. To top it all off was either a fresh cake or pie. Life was good.

I got to share a bed with my older cousin Tommy and listen to the train come by at eight, ten, and two a.m. My first night was kind of scary. The track was near the house and in the country, with nothing else around, a train is loud. When it came by, the whole room would shake. After one day of hard work, I am not sure I heard the train much. If I did, it was a relaxing sound, like rain falling on a tin roof.

Before that first day of work, Uncle Louis got a call that a bear had torn up a bee yard of his, so he decided to skip work the next day to hunt the bear. Since I grew up in Homerville, Uncle Louis used to call me "City Boy." I never quite understood that name, since Homerville only had about two thousand people, but he liked it and that was fine with me. Just keep the food and the pay coming, and he could call me whatever he wanted to.

I will never forget what he said when he got off the phone that night: "City Boy, you want to go hunt the bear with us tomorrow? I'll still pay you a full day's pay." Wow! I am now a paid hunter. I figured that was a promotion, and I hadn't even worked a day. I quickly said yes. So, off to bed Tommy and I went, and between the train and the anticipation of meeting a live, wild bear, I was a tad on the nervous side. I'm not sure I slept any that first night.

Early before the light of dawn, Uncle Louis stuck his head into Tommy's room and told us to get up. We were up and dressed in no time. Then we went to his gun closet. He took out two Browning automatic shotguns, one for him and one for Tommy. I got a single shot 12 gauge. Uncle Louis gave Tommy a handful of shells and handed me one shell. I was thinking, *Well, I'm young, they're older than me, and sons are more important than nephews, so that must be fair.* While I was thinking these thoughts, he handed me one more shell. I think it's a good rule of thumb when you go bear hunting to have two shells.

Without benefit of daylight, we were off in the truck to the swamp where the bee yard and probably the bear were. We traveled down a three path sand road, and when Uncle Louis stopped the truck he said, "City Boy, I want to let you out right here." I got out of the truck with my shotgun and two shells. "When it gets daylight, you get on the hill and be on the lookout for the bear. We'll let the dogs out on up here a-ways, and there's a good chance that bear will come to you." I was not sure that was good news.

Uncle Louis and Tommy drove off, leaving me feeling pretty lonely. At the break of day my first thought was, *Where's that hill he was talking about?* I didn't see any hills. There were none. I had seen hills in movies and on postcards, but there aren't any in South Georgia. All the land is flat and sandy. That fact had me a tad shaken: no hill.

I calmed down and reasoned to myself and decided just to stay in the spot where my uncle put me out. Just a little later, I heard the dogs chasing the bear, and darned if they weren't coming my way. I put the first shell in my gun and took the safety off. I was ready, but before the bear got to me, it changed directions. Amen!

I heard a few shots off in the distance, and soon afterwards, Uncle Louis came and got out of the truck. Tommy had killed the bear, and they wanted me to help get his body out of the swamp and into the truck. I said yes, but if I had known what was ahead, I would have played sick.

When we got as close to where the bear was as we could get in the pick-up, we walked into the woods and straight into a bay swamp with 50-foot-tall trees surrounded by water and the water covered by peat moss. Since I'd never been in a swamp, I thought you could walk on the peat moss. I took my first step and found myself in two feet of water, then, very quickly, three feet. I was getting concerned about snakes.

Neither Lewis and Clark, nor anyone else, had ever explored this virgin land, and I'm hoping I get home alive. Uncle Louis led the way, and that fact made me feel a little better. We went about 100 yards into the swamp, and the walk was not easy.

Now we're with Tommy and the dead bear. The adults talk it over, and they decided they had to leave the bear where he fell, but they would cut off his feet for Tommy to remember his first kill by. What a great plan. "City Boy, you can carry the feet back to the hill." At that moment I knew their definition of hill: land you could stand on above water.

So now I have four bear feet, trying to walk through peat moss and knee deep water. At this point, I had already been under water a few times, maybe as many as twenty. I was happy when I got back to the hill, until I realized I had lost two of the four bear feet. Actually, I knew; I just didn't care. When I told Tommy, he was kind and just smiled and told me it was not a problem. It didn't seem to bother Uncle Louis either, and I didn't get fired.

I am now ready to get bee stung and to work the next day from daylight to dark and eat Aunt Gladys' food. Being a paid bear hunter was not for me.

GRANDDAD RAULERSON

I must warn you; this is not a story for horse lovers. Or, it may be, depending on which horse you were riding in this story. Please, place yourself in the saddle and try to enjoy. I hope you have a better understanding of the way things were in the old days.

This story is about how people acted and reacted during the turn of the century from the 19th to the 20th. The events are true and while they are not set in the Wild West, it may seem like it. Again, read this story with an understanding of how life was back then, but is no more.

All the folks in Echols County knew my Uncle J.H. Raulerson as Junior. He was the last of eight Raulerson children and was named after my grandfather J.H. Raulerson. In his later years, Uncle J.H. was trying to catch me up on some family history, and he told me this story.

In 1884, my grandfather was nine years old, and he had a younger brother who was seven. Their parents had died, and there were no other family members for them to live with, so they stayed in homes that needed help with work. The older brother worked in the fields and woods at various trades and took care of his younger brother. Uncle J.H. said that his dad grew up quick and hard. I don't think any of us can truly relate to what these two children experienced.

Over time, my grandfather did well and ended up with a large farm and a family of eight children, including Uncle J.H. Hard work and hard experiences didn't kill him, but only made him stronger. He loved his children, but he never gave any of them any slack. When he spoke, they reacted.

As a boy, Granddad moved up the ranks of jobs, and at a very young age, he became a woods rider. It was his job to check on the workers in the woods to make sure the work was getting done. It was a top job for this part of the country at that time. He reported to the land owners, and Uncle J.H. said he was loyal to the owners and the workers. One man he worked for, who owned a lot of land, treated him like a brother. Loyalty and honesty were important. A man's word was the man.

One day the boss and my grandfather were riding the woods. The boss man had just bought an expensive, solid white horse, and he was very proud of him. The horse had one problem. He was a biter. He would try to bite anything that got near him, and he was successful fairly often.

This big landowner liked to pick at other people and play around, but my grandfather, having grown up so hard, was no picker or player. As the two were riding down the road, the boss pulled his horse over toward my grandfather's horse, and the biter barely missed. My grandfather stopped and cussed the boss out and told him that better not happen again.

The boss kind of smiled after the lecture, and they went on through the woods. A few miles later, the boss did it again. My grandfather again cussed him out and gave him this warning. "If that horse bites my horse, I'll either kill you or him." The boss backed off and smiled, and they continued to ride on down the path.

It happened again the third time. This time, the boss's horse did bite my grandfather's horse. Not a good situation now. My grandfather gets off his horse, walks over to the boss, and without a word, pulls his pistol and shoots the biter with the boss still in the saddle.

As the horse was falling, the boss was using some very strong cuss words going down to the ground. He got up and continued on and on, and then fired my grandfather on the spot. According to Uncle J.H., the man used every cuss word known at that time.

My grandfather calmly got back on his horse and started leaving, saying nothing. Then the boss started laughing and couldn't quit. "Help me get my saddle off the horse and give me a ride back home," he said to my grandfather. He did just that, so now they're riding on the same horse.

While they were riding, the man said he should have known what was going to happen. Later down the path, the boss asked, "Why didn't you shoot me instead of the horse?" Granddad replied that he should have shot him and felt bad about killing the horse. "But boss, you have kids and the horse don't."

The two men became closer than ever after that day, and the friendship between their families is still very strong.

QUILTS

When I visited my grandparents and other relatives years back as a child, I noticed some common elements to their homes that I still recall. Most of the homes were wood frame with wood shutters and screens on the windows. They had wood or gas stoves, and a few of the houses had electricity, but most didn't.

The yards were sandy and bare, and the family swept them, since there was nothing to mow. Everyone had a well with a hand pump to supply water, and the outhouse was built away from the well. The women liked flowers planted near the home, and there were always animals around: dogs, cats, horses, cows, chickens, goats—you name it.

At my grandparents' home, I remember the sugar cane mill and cook kettle, and I was fascinated with the smoke house where meat was seasoned and cured. I have always thought that if I won the lottery, I would get a personal smoke house.

My family would kill their hogs during the coldest part of the winter, smoke and cure the meat with salt, and let it hang in the smoke house until it was ready to eat. I'm sure there were other steps taken to keep the meat safe to eat, but I have no clue as to what those steps were.

My grandfather worked his farm with a mule and plow and a hand hoe. If the family didn't work, they didn't eat. There was no grocery store in the swamp woods where they lived. I remember the rolling truck that came by once a week. That's what we called it: the rolling truck.

It brought sugar, meal, flour, coffee, ice and items of that nature. They also had crackers and candy.

I have found that grandparents of that day and this day have something in common. They can't say no to a grandkid who wants a candy bar.

Most of the homes I remember from my childhood had large oak trees around the home, so the heat of summer and bugs weren't too bad. With the wood shutters open and screens on the windows, the homes were pleasant during the summer. I never remember being very hot in any of my relatives' or friends' homes.

Now I want to share with you what I thought was the greatest creation of all during this time period of the 1950s: the quilt. Most of the wood homes had tin roofs and no insulation. I have heard stories of folks comparing the homes they grew up in to those of their neighbors.

One man said he was so poor that their wood floor had cracks in it big enough to drop feed to the chickens through the floor. A friend of his said that was nothing. The holes in their floor were so big that the chickens could eat right out of your hand.

The first fellow said, "We had holes in our tin roof, and you could see the stars through them." Not to be outdone, the second man said, "That's nothing. The holes in our roof were so big, you could see the full moon through them." So, now I'm ready to journey with you to see what a winter night was like in these homes.

During the winter nights when we went to bed, the air inside ranged from chilly to very cold. With just one fireplace in the whole house, getting the rooms warm was a losing proposition. If the man of the house didn't get up and put wood on the fire during the night, it got really bad. With the freezing cold, we would have frozen to death if not for the quilts. I love quilts.

I especially remember two freezing cold nights when I was a child. The first time was at my grandparents' home. That night the large home was super cold, even with my grandfather feeding the fireplace new wood off and on all night. I came close to freezing, and some quilts saved my life.

The second occasion was at my Uncle Jessie B.'s home in the little crossroads of Withers. It was another cold night, and my uncle and dad had a tad too much shine that evening. That meant no firewood was added to the fire during the cold night, as both men slept in peace. Thank goodness Dad had tucked me in under several quilts prior to his last drink. Once again, I was thankful that we had quilts. I love quilts. Without a doubt, they saved my life more than once. Life was good, but cold at times.

THE BUS

Here's another Haylow story to share with you. To go to school, we kids had to ride the school bus from Haylow to Statenville and then return that afternoon to Haylow. It was about a thirty minute ride, so we were up early and home late.

The rides were hot and dirty. Have you ever seen school pictures of kids from the 1950s? Even after a good bath from the wash pot on the back porch that morning and maybe a granny haircut, we got dirty pretty fast. Those haircuts were bad, all gapped up. Also, maybe wearing the same clothes a few times each week before the clothing got really dirty had something to do with the bad pictures.

We had to wash our own clothes in the wash pot on the back porch, ring them out by hand, and hang them on the porch to dry. Hey, and I was only a second grader at that time. Life is not always fair.

No iron touched our clothes after they dried. Remember, we didn't have irons or the electricity to run them. That was one more good reason to get three good days of wear before rewashing. With this approach, your clothes were wrinkle-free about the third day you wore them.

Plus, we did not have to wear shoes to school. You were not in the in-group if you wore shoes during the summer. When my mom insisted I wear my shoes, I would hide them on the way to school and put them back on when I headed home. We were a rough-looking bunch of kids, with dirty clothes and dirty feet for sure.

Today, during our modern times of No Child Getting Left Behind policy and our government's view of children, DFCS certainly would have taken over almost all of us in those days, but they were not around then. Good news for society: we all turned out pretty good and now wear shoes all the time.

I guess at the time if DFCS had been around, most of us would have been sent elsewhere, likely to schools in Valdosta. Valdosta was the city and still is. You had to wear shoes there. Going to school so far away would have meant an hour ride to school with bus changes involved for all of us.

Good ole days, maybe so or maybe not. At least in South Georgia we didn't have to walk two miles to school in the snow as our north Georgia mates did. We got to ride on a hot dirty road in a bus.

One plus was that on Tuesdays, our bus driver would stop at the gas station in Statenville for us to buy a candy bar. Life was good if we had money to get a treat, which most of the time we did. I can't recall the driver's name, but he made sure we all got candy. Now we are talking real kindness. I still love Tuesdays.

MERRY GO ROUND

In 1957 I was in the second grade in Statenville, Georgia. I'm sure the county's school had to be one of the smallest in the state, since Echols County had the lowest population of the 159 counties.

When I think back to that time in my life, two thoughts come to mind very quickly. One was going home to eat lunch. The second thought is about the school's merry-go-round.

The first thing I recall was being allowed to walk home for lunch if you lived close to the school. At that time my mom and dad were separated, and she had rented a house nearby. I had a block or so walk, and then I was home for lunch.

My mother had my favorite meal of all time cooked each day: a juicy, fried hamburger, fresh homemade French fries, and a large glass of chocolate milk. I think she was trying to keep me buttered up, because the first chance I had to go back to my dad, I was gone.

The second thing I remembered about that year was the circular, push merry-go-round on the school grounds. It would hold about ten kids on the seats, and the larger kids, fourth grade and older, would get in the middle and push it. It would go so fast that you learned quickly to hold on tight, or you would fly off. I rode it one time per week on average, and each time I would be dizzy and sick on my stomach.

My last time on the merry-go-round is a day I will never forget. That day we were short one of the larger boys to help push on the inside. They needed one more pusher, and it was me. The bigger boys did not take kindly to the word no, so, I am now inside to help push. I was scared.

In just a few seconds the contraption was moving. Shortly, we were flying. It was like holding onto an airplane taking off. At that point, my feet were not even touching the ground. I am in a superman position, holding on to the merry-go-round with my legs and feet straight out behind me.

I started praying my first prayer. "God, save my life." As the merry-go-round spun, I was holding on for dear life, and I didn't feel merry. I knew if my hands came off the bar, I would be dead. But, God spared me. The big boys finally started slowing down the ride, and I held on to the end. I had blisters, stomach problems, and the world was swimming around. The good news: I did as the big boys told me, and I was alive.

My last merry-go-round ride was in 1957. God was good. Life is good.

THE ALLEN FAMILY TREE

I am proud that my grandparents were south Georgians. Echols county and Clinch county were their worlds. A few things both sets of my grandparents had in common were growing up poor, working hard, and having lots of children.

My grandparents wanted to see each of their children inherit a better life than they had. That was their dream. They wanted their children to move out of poverty. I'm sure the children were not spared the whip, and they learned to work from an early age.

At that time, in the early 1900s, education was not a major factor in their lives. They all got a hard-knock education in survival by having solid values and working hard from my grandparents' perspective.

In this story I will focus on my dad's side of the family. I have lots of stories about my grandparents on the Raulerson side of the family, but nothing much about the Allen side. The main reason is by the time I was born, my dad's parents had already died. Two of my dad's brothers and one of his sisters were deceased by the time I was very old. I have first cousins from those uncles and aunt who are much older than me, and I have no clue who they are.

My dad's father's name was Elzie B. Allen, born in 1876. His nickname was "Coote." I'm not sure if that was a good nickname or not. My grandmother's name was Fannie McClain Allen. She was born in 1880. With the name Fannie, she didn't need a nickname.

Two other family nicknames that stand out to me are my Uncle Flynn's, (Brother) and Uncle Vernie's (Somebody). I guess Brother's nickname was easy for his siblings to remember. I can hear the family calling Vernie's name: "Somebody, come home!" And I guess Somebody did.

Likewise, I had a nickname. Thank goodness I lost it when I started school. It was Sambo. Later it changed to Jimbo and then to Jimmy.

Of all my relatives whom I never had the chance to meet, I would have loved to spend some time with Somebody (Uncle Vernie). It was my understanding that he was one of my grandparents' favorite children. He was born in 1920 and died in 1943 at the young age of 23.

Uncle Vernie had just returned from fighting in Europe in World War II. During his second week home, he was accidently killed by a train. Somebody had decided to jump on the train from Haylow to Valdosta, a common way for young men to travel in those days.

I was told he had a little too much to drink before taking the leap toward the train, and he fell under it. Somebody's death at age twenty-three was a hard loss for our family, especially since he died just a few hundred yards from his parent's home after making it through a war thousands of miles away.

This story reminds me of the sacrifices our veterans have made for this country and of the lives they try to rebuild when they return home wounded in more ways than meets the eye. Many of our veterans, who make it back, die in battles to restart their lives here at home. They are heroes, too, and we need to remember and honor them.

I am very proud of my family tree on both sides and how each generation worked hard to make it better for the next. In America we need to return to the strong family values and the hard work of my grandparents' generation.

CLINCH COUNTY

Most of my stories are from Clinch County and Homerville, so for many of my friends who know nothing about this county, I have researched some facts and will share them with you. Maybe this information will help you have a better understanding of South Georgia and Clinch County.

Homerville is the county seat. The town was once a stagecoach drop off and was incorporated in 1869. The county was established in 1850. Clinch county was named after General Duncan Clinch, who was credited with the defeat of Seminole Chief Osceola in 1812.

Clinch was the first home of the Oconee Indians and one of the counties where the Okefenokee Swamp is located. Highways 441 and 84 are the crossroads in the middle of town. Valdosta and Waycross are larger area cities.

The county is one of the smaller populated counties in Georgia, but it is the third largest in geographical size in the state with over 800 square miles of land. The main industries through the years have been turpentine, logging, saw mills, and honey production. More recently it has become one of the larger blueberry-producing counties in the nation. One of the oldest buildings still being used is the courthouse, which was built in 1895.

When I finished high school in 1968, the county population was about 5,000 people. It's now over 7,000. In the 1960s, the county car license tag number was 144 out of 159 Georgia counties. In those days as you traveled around the state, you could tell other people's home county by the first three numbers on the license plate. I miss those days.

I used to tell folks, "You can tell who's from Clinch County, because we all have water stain marks on our legs from standing in swamp water." We were so far back in the country, we couldn't listen to the Grand Ole Opry on Saturday nights. It took the air waves 'til Monday to get to us.

Clinch county has lots of land and more good folks per acre than anywhere else in Georgia.

MAIL ROUTE

Before I started to school, my dad had a job as a rural mail carrier. His route was from Haylow to the southern side of Fargo, Georgia. Each day, he would drive about two hundred miles over dirt roads. There were only about thirty houses on his route, so we made few stops, and I had lots of time with my dad.

I was small, and I would sit on top of the money box next to him as we traveled those roads. All we ever saw were pine trees, gall berries, wild hogs, and deer. We listened to country music on his radio the whole day long. I can't sing one of those songs or remember any of the words after hours of listening to country music each day. I think that was one of those gifts from birth that I missed, but I was next to my dad for the day, and life was good.

My dad and I were the only people most of those folks saw each day, other than their family members. They were some lonely folks. We are talking backwoods. I can't even imagine what their lives were like day to day. But one thing for certain, they were the salt of the earth and would do anything they could for you.

Most of the time, someone from each house would be waiting on Dad at the mailbox. He would turn the car off and visit. Time was no factor. Often, we would go in the houses and eat breakfast here and there and then lunch later on. Some folks would even share a drink of shine now and then. Not for me, but for my dad.

Also, my dad was the carrier of messages from one house to another and the bearer of the local news. He was the voice. These homes did not get newspapers, some didn't have radios, and for certain there were no telephones or televisions on his route.

Maybe half of the folks on the mail route didn't have transportation, so when asked, he would give them rides going forward on his route. Often, he would come back when he finished his job and take them where they needed to go. He was a free taxi service as he worked his route.

Some days Dad would pack us a lunch of saltine crackers, sardines, Vienna sausage, and a cold Coke from Aunt Gladys's iced-down drink box. We would park the car and just walk in the woods to find a clear spot on the ground. We'd sit and lean back against some pine trees, say grace, and eat. Life was good.

I know all of you reading this story would have loved to experience a few days on Dad's mail route. Here was the real fun of why I loved to go with him. When people needed anything for their homes or farms, guess where it came from? It was not Wal-Mart. Correct answer: Sears and Roebuck. Did you make the right guess? Yes, people in the country ordered all they needed from the seasonal catalogues, except food: Clothing, pots, pans, pumps, nails, screws, and the list goes on.

On the days when these items were expected to arrive, people would come running down the road toward our car when they saw the dust rising out on the road. I especially liked it when someone had ordered baby chicks, biddies we called them. They would be only a few days old and about twenty-four in a box. They looked sad, and I took it upon myself to try to cheer them up. I would take them in the back seat, and we had a great time. We sang, listened to the radio, and talked trash while my dad drove us down the road. It was a great time together. Yes, life was good.

THE COGDELL SPOOK LIGHT

Everyone who grew up in Clinch County knew the tales of the spook light in Cogdell. The town was a small community consisting of a few homes, a general store, the post office, and...the light!

The tale was that when the railroad was being built through Cogdell, a conductor was trying to stop the train with his lantern one night, and he was hit by the train and killed. His ghost, they say, is still waving his lantern, trying to stop that ghost train. I know you doubt that story, but when I was a teenager, it sounded pretty right to me.

Going to see the Cogdell spook light became a social event in our county. Hay rides, car loads of teenagers looking for a thrill, or couples looking for an excuse to go parking and sparking were all reasons to go to Cogdell.

I had been to the area many times from about the seventh grade into high school, but I had never seen the spook light. I didn't believe there was one. I would hear my friends tell about seeing the light and how it scared the mess out of them, but I was skeptical. I'm pretty sure I didn't see it because of the quietness factor. They said you had to be totally quiet, or it wouldn't appear, and silence was not one of my strong suits at that time in my life.

To see the light, you had to drive down a certain dirt road, cross a wooden bridge, turn around and go back across the bridge, turn your car and headlights off, then be quiet and look back toward Cogdell. If you were positioned just right, you could barely see a street light in the distant town.

One night I took a friend's cousin (girl) to see the light after a movie. I did all the steps correctly. It was very dark and quiet in the car. We waited maybe five minutes, and then I whispered, "Do you see a smaller light next to the Cogdell street light?"

She did. We froze and kept watching, and the smaller light gradually increased in size, growing from candle light to the size of a basketball in just a few minutes. The thing was coming our way!

As it got closer, it was kind of hazy looking, like a cloud. In another five minutes, the light was the size of a car and still coming to us. We both hollered, and I cranked up the car. Turning on the headlights and blowing the horn, I started driving toward the light, and it was gone.

I had heard that if you stayed quiet, the light would come right through your car, but I was not interested in that experience. To this day, I have no clue as to where that light came from or what caused it, but I did see the light. My date did, too, and she never came back to Homerville.

Famous Clinch County People

The best people in the world lived in the county I grew up in. We did have some in the jail house, and a few made their living moonshining, but that didn't make them all bad. Okay, we did have an occasional murder, but the shooter's defense was usually that they were shooting to miss. They were just trying to scare someone who needed scaring, not kill them.

I could name a hundred famous people from Homerville that were great and kind people that you might not have heard of. They were famous in many ways to me and to other people who knew them. However, I can think of four of our folks who did make headlines outside the county, so I will go with those famous four for now. My Homerville friends may add to this list.

The first was Miss Georgia, 1960: Miss Sandy Talley. She was older than me, and she once came to school to see her mom, Mrs. Talley, my fourth grade teacher. I was in class that day she walked in and, WOW, one pretty girl!

Sandy Talley represented Clinch County well, and how lucky could a girl be: She once had lunch with Fireball Roberts, a famous racecar driver of the day.

The second famous person from Clinch County made it into the Ripley's Believe It Or Not book. His name was 5/8 Smith. Ripley's said, jokingly, that he was not a whole man, just 5/8.

Mr. Smith was born in DuPont, Georgia in 1912, the son of a man named Frank Smith who was fed up with being mistaken for other men with the same name. There were five other Frank Smiths in DuPont alone. When his son was born, Mr. Frank sat down and considered the problem of being a Smith with a common first name. He thought of all the confusion and embarrassment he had suffered because of his name.

The more he thought about it, the more determined he became that his son should have a name the likes of which no other mortal on earth possessed or was likely ever to possess. In the end, Frank chose to name his son 5/8. Not spelled out like Five-Eighths, but 5/8 Smith.

The third famous person from Clinch County was the actor, Ossie Davis. He was born in, of all places, Cogdell, Georgia. At that time, Cogdell had a population of maybe 100 folks. He made a big mark on Hollywood in the movies and was also seen often on TV and on Broadway. Mr. Davis was a writer, director, and actor, and he did well in life.

The fourth famous Clinch Countian is a lady named Jolene Ammons. She was a professional basketball player, who played for the All-American Redheads. I was lucky enough to see her play, and boy was she great! Ms. Ammons played for the Redheads for twelve seasons. They played men's amateur teams all across America, and the team's record was 1,848 wins and 468 losses.

In her career, Jolene Ammons scored over 25,000 points, and when she played, they didn't have a three-point range to shoot from. During her career, she was highlighted on many national television shows. She is also a Facebook friend of mine, so send her a note to say hello.

Yep, I am proud of my county and the famous people it has produced.

A SOUTH GEORGIA
BOY'S LIFE

THREE'S A CROWD

When I was growing up, two of my best friends were my neighbors. Danny Ray lived across the street, Wink lived behind our house, and we were all about the same age. I seemed to have always known these two. They were like family.

We would spend hours playing and staying together. Most of the time we got along perfectly, but not all the time. As long as the combination was just two, life was good. Danny Ray and Wink were first cousins, but that relationship didn't really affect our play time. What affected it was when the three of us were all together. We would have fun for a while, but then one had to go. Some days it was me. Other days it was one of them. I'm not sure how we decided to team up or who had to go, but it just worked out that way.

One day that still lingers in my head was a day that Wink had to go. We had been playing in my back yard and then Danny Ray or I told Wink to go home. He didn't want to go. At that time I had a BB gun. You can see trouble coming. I told Danny Ray to shoot Wink if he didn't go. Wink was a brave one. He stood there. Then Danny Ray asked me where to shoot him. I said the foot. I am not sure what I was thinking or if I was thinking. Danny Ray shot Wink in the foot, and I was shocked.

Wink started crying, a little at first, and then he took off running to his house and crying big time. He wasn't really hurt that bad, but he wanted some attention.

Oops! Danny Ray started running to his house, and I decided it would be a good time to go in mine. I think we knew what lay ahead for us. Sure enough, when I got in the house, the party line phone rang. It was for Danny Ray's home: one ring. Ours was two rings. Across the road I heard noise, and it was Danny Ray pleading for mercy. There was none.

My mom was home, but at that point, our phone hadn't rung. Since I was not the shooter, I reasoned that maybe Wink's mom wouldn't call mine. Darn! Guess what? I heard two rings on the party line. My mom answered. I could hear enough to know she was hotter than a firecracker.

I did get what I deserved, and it wasn't pleasant.

Somehow through the years after that day, we managed not to have any more shootings and played pretty well together, even the three of us. Life is good.

How They Avoided Spankings

As I was growing up, there were two kids I observed who used different approaches to avoid spankings. Sometimes they were successful and sometimes they weren't, but they used the same approach each time.

The first kid was my sister Sonja. She was a few years older than me and seldom got in trouble, but when she did, it set our mom off big time.

When Sonja saw Mom coming with a belt or a switch, she would start running around the house. She was in better condition than Mom and could stay ahead of her pretty well. I liked watching them make laps around the house. Mom would soon run out of breath, quit the chase, and promise not to spank Sonja if she would just come inside and quit making fools of both of them. Mom lied.

When Mom spanked Sonja once or twice after promising not to, my sister caught on and kept her distance till the next day. By then, Mom would have calmed down, so Sonja's method got to where it worked pretty good.

The second offender was my neighbor Danny Ray. He and I were about the same age, and his family lived right across the street from us. His adventures were a lot more fun to watch than my sister's. His dad, who we all called Uncle Haskell, was half the action. We were not related, but all the kids in our neighborhood called all the adults Aunt or Uncle.

Uncle Haskell was one of my all-time favorite Homerville people.

When in trouble, Danny Ray's approach was to run for the pecan tree in his back yard. Uncle Haskell always had a belt and was just a few steps behind him. One was hollering for the other one to stop, and the other one was always crying at the top of his lungs. Danny Ray always won the race to the tree.

It seemed like when Danny Ray grabbed the first limb, he was somehow at the top of that thirty-foot tree in a matter of seconds. All of the neighborhood kids gathered to see what would happen next.

Uncle Haskell couldn't climb the tree, and Danny Ray couldn't stay there forever. So we thought. It had been told that he had once spent the night in the tree. Most of the time, they talked back and forth to each other with little or no agreement. Poor Danny Ray's approach never worked. As soon as he came down from the tree, it happened.

Looking back, I'm not sure why he headed to the same tree each time he got into trouble, always with the same results.

ORANGES WERE MADE TO EAT (NOT TO THROW)

One evening right before dark, my neighborhood friends, Danny Ray and Wink and I came up with a plan. Well, we didn't have a plan actually. It kind of just took hold one step at a time. We were pre-teens at the time in Homerville, and I guess we just wanted to be bad. I blame Danny Ray as the one who influenced us to make bad choices that night.

The first bad choice was to get some oranges off Fred Landrum's front porch. After we ate a few, we still had two or three each. Then, either Danny Ray or Wink suggested we go downtown and climb up on Homerville Supply's roof to see if we could hit a truck coming through town. Wink's father owned the hardware store, and we meant no harm in our actions. We were just looking for some small town fun.

We sneaked off downtown, and the climb to the top of the two-story building was not easy. We finally made it to the top of the store, and it was dark by then. A few trucks came by, and we tossed oranges at them with no hits. I am sure it was Wink who saw a pulpwood truck coming, and he let one go toward the truck. The throw was a perfect hit on the driver's door. When the orange hit, it sounded like a shotgun blast.

The driver stopped on the spot and got out of the truck, and when he did, I saw the largest man I had ever seen in my life. Hulk Hogan looked small in comparison. I was frozen, afraid to move. What if he saw us? I heard a sound behind me and turned around in time to see my friends leaving the scene.

Danny Ray and Wink were at the back of the building, and when I got back there, they had already jumped off the top of a twenty foot high building and were running home. I am now alone, the last man at the scene of the crime. I tried to climb down, but was going slow, so I decided to jump the rest of the way.

When I hit the ground, my knees hit my chin and flipped me backwards. I was still able to get up and run as fast as I could toward home. I finished the trip in record time, made sure all the doors were locked, and went straight to bed. I said my prayers, praying mainly that the driver of that truck hadn't followed me.

It was a good feeling to wake up the next day and be alive. That same morning, I vowed to only eat oranges and drink orange juice from then on, and never to throw one at anything. Mr. Pulpwood Man, if you are reading this story, please forgive us. If you can't let it go, now that I think about it, Danny Ray made the suggestion to throw oranges at trucks, and Wink is the one who hit your truck. I was just there.

Roy Rogers

Many years back, I could not get any of my friends to believe this story, but I will try again. I'm not sure you'll believe it either, but it did happen, so here goes. I sure wish I'd had a phone with a camera in it back then.

I was not yet going to school and on weekdays I would spend a lot of time at my dad's gas station in Homerville. All of my friends were either in the first or second grade. Oh, how I miss the old gas station.

Folks would stop and get gas, and since this time was before fast food places, they would get cold drinks, peanuts, or crackers. The best sellers were weenies or baloney from the meat display case along with a loaf of bread. Other top sellers were saltine crackers, Vienna sausage, and cans of sardines.

Dad had a charge account set up for local folks and many times he charged gas to people who were just passing through and didn't have enough money, but promised to mail him the money. He could not say no, so he would write them out a ticket. My uncle, J.H. Raulerson, who worked at the station, told me years later that when Dad closed the station, he had over $10,000 in credit notes he never collected. I guess I'm different from my dad in that sense. I can say no. I'm not sure if that ability is good or bad.

One hot summer day at the station across the street from Dad's station, a large semi truck pulled in for gas. The trailer was painted with pictures of Bullet and Trigger, with Roy Rogers, King of the Cowboys, written on the side in big letters. Then, out from the driver's side steps the man himself: Roy Rogers. I was in shock.

"Hello, Roy!" I yelled, and I waved. He waved back and said hello to me. To ME! Roy Rogers! I just watched as he filled his truck up, and in a few minutes he was gone. I have often wondered why I didn't cross the street to shake hands with him. He was my hero and still is. Darn! I did wave bye again to him, and he waved back.

I ran home to tell all the kids my news, but no one believed me, and I had no proof. I'm telling you, I did see Roy Rogers in Homerville. What a day! Life is good.

THE POOL

When I was in the sixth grade, it cost one quarter to go swimming all day at the city pool in Homerville. It opened at 1 p.m. and closed at 6. The pool was the best life had to offer in those days: a cold swim in a hot summer with friends. I was not much into girls at the time, but there were always plenty of them at the pool, and most of the boys in town were there, too. It was the place to be.

I learned to swim at the city pool. I loved to do laps both under and on top of the water. I'd race across the pool with anyone there. I may have even set a few unrecorded swimming records between us kids back then. We had a first class pool with a diving board.

One thing I was not good at was diving. I could do a jack knife, a straight dive, and a cannon ball. Many of the daily swimmers would do a full flip or more off the board. I could never make it around fast enough and would always hit flat on my back. It hurt, but I was a big boy and didn't cry... often. I would always try each day, though. The results were always the same: a blistered back with never a complete rotation.

I was a failure in life, but I tried. I may even hold the record for attempts.

Only two things would have kept me away from the pool. One was lightning and the other was the lack of a quarter. The good news was that I had a bike with a basket on the handlebars. I usually started out with just a penny that I had found on the ground. Even now, I can't walk past a penny without picking it up. Maybe somewhere in my head, I'm thinking of how important this find was in my past life.

At that time I was thinking that I only needed 24 more cents to be able to swim that day. Within a few hours each day, I had my quarter. All I had to do was ride down the Fargo highway and pick up soda bottles. Then I took them to Chauncey's grocery store, and Mr. Everyl would pay me two cents per bottle returned. Bingo! I had my money. Swimming pool, I was headed your way. All I needed was 12 bottles a day to enjoy the good life.

A Blast in Homerville

John Barrett was one of my top friends in Homerville. He was the son of Reverend Paul Barrett who was my minister at the Methodist Church. When I was growing up, I spent many hours at their home, enjoying the fellowship there immensely.

Some lessons were learned at their home that had nothing to do with the Bible, and one of those was learned by John himself. In our preteen years fireworks were in, big time. Kids would come to school telling stories about what a "cannon ball" or M80 would do to a tin can or an apple. I was not into fireworks myself, thank goodness. After a near-death experience, John gave them up, too. The brush he had with death was not from a cannon ball, but from his mom.

One evening after school, John had bought a few cannon balls and was having fun blowing stuff up before his parents got home. He was down to his last one and had just lit it when he saw his Mom coming home. He quickly put the fuse out with his fingers and ran into the house to hide the powerful firecracker.

He panicked, and the first good hiding place he saw was the sugar bowl. His plan was to remove it from the bowl once his mom went to another room. Good plan. John and I graduated together, and he was the top student in our class. He was smart, so the plan should work.

His mom came into the house, and they spoke for a while. Before she could go to another room, an ember on the fuse relit the cannon ball in the sugar bowl. John said it sounded like a bomb going off in the

49

house. Glass and sugar went everywhere, and the noise scared John and his mother half to death.

After he confessed, he got it from both parents and spent the rest of the evening cleaning up glass and sugar. This story reminds me of a popular song back then: "Sugar, Sugar."

Later, John's dad was assigned to another church, and they moved. It's said you can still find sugar in the cracks and crevices of that home. I'm glad that John and his mom survived the Homerville blast.

A Bad Memory

Many years back, when I was in the sixth grade, we had a class bully. He was tough on the playground, and it was better that you be on his side, than to disagree with him. A few times he and I did disagree. We would settle our differences with some form of a tussle.

I lost one round, and he lost one during that time. It was for sure that after the bouts, a paddling would come our way. But, he did realize that after those fights, I was no push over, and maybe I gained a little respect from him. We then became kind of friends.

I sometimes think about him and what happened to him one day in our classroom. After all these years, I still have bad thoughts about the incident, and I think about the differences between education now compared to then.

We had a great teacher that year, but sometimes the best of teachers have enough from big-mouthed, disrespectful kids. As they say, the crap then hits the fan, and I was there when it hit.

That particular day my maybe friend had upset the teacher. She had enough. She called him to the front of the classroom. She told him to go to the chalkboard and get a piece of chalk. I was wondering what in the world was going to happen. The bully did as the teacher requested.

"Mr. Smarty Britches," she said, "I want you to show the class just how smart you are." He stood there, and we could tell that he wondered what was coming. We were all watching in suspense. Then the teacher told him to write his name on the blackboard.

There was silence. I'm certain there were tears in his eyes as the boy told the teacher that he didn't know how to write his name. I know there were tears in my eyes. She then told him to go back to his desk and to behave.

My heart hurt for him that day, and it still does. I have no clue how a kid can get to the sixth grade or even the second and not know how to write his name.

I know that my thoughts and this story will have no bearing on educational leaders, but why in the heck wasn't he taught to write his name? I have no problem with kids staying behind until they can perform certain minimal education skills. If they can't perform, put them in a non-graded math, reading, or writing class until they can do the work.

I once heard a story of a guy quitting school in the sixth grade, and someone asked him why he quit. He said he had caught up to his dad and didn't want to pass him. There is no shame in getting left behind, but there is shame when you can't write your name. I know. I saw it. The bully and I both lived through it that day in the sixth grade.

STILL MAD

I guess I need to get over it, but every now and then when I see a twenty dollar bill, it happens. I get a little mad at, of all people, my MOM. Yes, she birthed me, fed me, and generally did the best she could to rear me. I know I need to grow up, be mature, forgive, and go on with life, but it's just hard at times. I'll tell you the story, and you decide.

Have you ever thought of how much money you need to be happy? When I was in the sixth grade, I had a paper route. After school each day, regardless of the weather, I would ride my bike about ten miles around Homerville to deliver the Waycross Journal-Herald. I had about sixty homes I would take the paper to each day. On a good week, after paying for the papers and collecting money on Saturday mornings, I would average about six dollars profit for the week.

When you ride one hundred miles per week on a bike, you have plenty of time to daydream. I loved to daydream on my bike, and my dream was to be rich one day. The amount I needed to be rich was twenty dollars. I could get a new baseball glove, a Yankee baseball cap, and I could enjoy a foot long hot dog and large root beer at the Triangle Food Shop in the middle of town with the rest of the money for a few weeks. Maybe I could even quit my job.

As I was delivering papers one day, I saw a twenty dollar bill next to Highway 441 North, on the edge of a yard. The money was five feet from the road and 150 feet from the nearest home. Life was good. Of course, I stopped, picked up the money, and put it in my pocket. Did I say life was good?

As I was heading home, the thought occurred to me that I needed to tell my mom I had found twenty dollars. If I didn't tell her, she would question my new life of luxury. Mom, guess what I found today. I then told her that I had found a twenty dollar bill. She should have just left the matter there, but she didn't. The questions started coming. In the end, she was not happy. She told me to go back to the closest house and see if they had lost any money, and if so, return it.

Mom said, "Most likely, and I'm not calling names, but the man of the house was bad to drink, and the money probably fell out of his pocket."

"Mom," I said, "it was next to the highway."

"Take it back." End of discussion.

The next day, I went to the home and knocked on the door. The lady of the house comes to the door, wondering what I'm doing there. I told her that as I rode my bike by yesterday, I found some money in her front yard.

"If you can tell me the amount, I'll return it."

She paused. "I'm not sure of the amount, but most likely my husband dropped it when he got out of his truck, and the wind blew it to the road. I'm not sure of the amount."

I had heard enough. I handed her the twenty dollar bill and left. She didn't even give me a thank you or a twenty-five cent reward. Some days it's just hard to say life is good. That day was one of them. Mom, I'm still trying to get over my loss of the high life.

SCHOOL IN (OF ALL PLACES) DUPONT

When I was growing up in the 1950s, Clinch County had elementary schools in Homerville and Fargo. The junior high schools were in Dupont and Fargo. The high school was in Homerville.

The Dupont School was very small and isolated with only six teachers and one principal. Going to school there was kind of like being in prison. We kids would board the bus in Homerville each morning, ride the ten miles to Dupont for school, and then return in the afternoon.

Little did I realize how my life would be transformed during those two years of junior high. We heard that the school board had hired a new principal from Alabama that year to be in charge of the Dupont School. I can't find words to describe him, but maybe as the story goes on in more detail, you will understand more about Mr. Lloyd Mims.

It is now the first day of school in Dupont for me as a seventh grader. Three loads of kids, including me, pile off the buses laughing and having fun. We are all in front of the school building when the man dashes out and loses his cool, demanding in an angry, high voice for all of us to shut up. The only sounds you could hear then were the beating of several hundred terrified hearts.

He then informed us of some of his rules: be quiet at all times, pay attention to the teachers, and walk on the right side of the hall when classes change. He then told the teachers to place any student that caused trouble in the hallway. He would check the halls every once in a while, and anyone the teachers put in the hall would get a paddling.

Mr. Mims was good for his word. One time when a teacher sent me to the hall, I tried to blend into the wood. It didn't work. He saw me, paddled me, and then sent me back to class. His temper was shorter than a burned-out candle.

The next day my friend, Orrin Deason, and I were in the bathroom. We had finished our business, washed our hands, and on the way out, we thought it would be fun to play tag. Mr. Mims met us at the door, and he was hot. We didn't think playing tag was anywhere close to murder, so we didn't understand why he was so worked up. He took his belt off and gave us a few swipes. At this point, I wasn't sure I would survive two years at this school.

Then, to make matters worse, Mr. Mims became my English teacher. In his class you either did everything he said in a timely way, or you would get a paddling. I tried my best to behave, but on some days, I thought it would be best to wear two pair of jeans.

I was not the best English student in the class. If Mr. Mims gave us the definition of a verb to learn for homework and to repeat in class the next day, I usually ended up with a paddling for noncompliance. I was not good at English, but between his way of teaching and the paddlings, I did make progress. I also started learning how to behave.

Even though he was very strict and hard-nosed, I ended up liking him in a strange way. Maybe it was because he would let some of us boys eat left-overs in the lunch room or because he encouraged me to be good at sports on the playground. Once, he even gave me an A in public speaking. We had to go on the stage, and using note cards, talk for three minutes. I thought I would die. Babe Ruth was my topic the day I got the A.

I was very happy when I graduated from the eighth grade the next year. I was now leaving Dupont for good, and I was high school bound. It was a great day to graduate. Good-by, Mr. Mims. Life is good.

The next year I went into the ninth grade at the high school in Homerville. It was the best year of my life. However, going into the tenth grade the next year, we found out that Mr. Mims was going to be the new high school principal. I cried. I'll continue this story related to my high school years and Mr. Mims in a later tale.

LOVE FOR A DAY

I'm not sure if this love was my first or not. It could have been, but it's kind of hard to decide, even fifty years later. I'll tell the story, and you help me decide.

I was in the seventh grade, and a girl named Rita asked me to sit with her on the bus ride to school that morning. She was an older woman: eighth grade. All I remember thinking is that maybe she was the one.

At school that day, they were showing a movie, and she asked me to sit with her, so I did. The auditorium was dark, and when they started the movie, she reaches over and wants to hold my hand. Why not, I thought. At our school, if you were caught holding hands, you got a paddling, so that was a pretty good reason not to. After about twenty minutes of holding hands, I'm thinking a paddling might have been a better alternative. What was the point?

It is now time to head back home on the bus. She again asks me to sit with her going back to Homerville from the Dupont School. Once we get there, the bus stops, and when we get off, I hear someone call her name. "Rita, over here!" I look in that direction, and a soldier is heading our way. I will say that again. An Army soldier in uniform is heading our way. They hug, and off they go in his car. I didn't even get a wave goodbye.

I'm now walking home wondering what just happened. That love-in-process deal had a quick death. The next day I'm again sitting on my bus with my buddies, Orrin and John. Life is back to normal, and I'm no longer heartbroken.

Rita and I did not cross paths much after that. Years later I heard that she and the soldier ended up marrying and living happily afterwards. I was kind of glad the romance ended on day one. Holding hands and breaking school rules was not my cup of tea.

Life is good.

To Lie or Not to Lie

Ms. Talley was my fourth grade teacher. At the time I was going to school in Homerville, but the next year I would transfer to Valdosta. She was soft-spoken and easy going, and I thought she was close to being a perfect teacher.

One thing I loved about her class was a multiplication game we played. Someone would stand next to their desk, and Mrs. Talley would ask, "What are nine times eight?" The first one to answer seventy-two would get to advance to the next desk. One of my goals in class was to make it all the way around and not have to sit down before I got back to my desk. It wasn't an easy achievement, because we had some smart students in my class, but I did make it all the way around the class a few times. Life is good.

At that time I loved math and most of the time I did my homework and was a pretty good student. I'm not sure what happened to Ms. Talley this one particular day. She asked us to get out our math homework, and she found out that most of us hadn't done it. She became mad and upset. That was the first time I had seen her that way.

Then, out of the blue, she picked up her paddle. I sat on the last row going left to right. She went to the first row on the left and started checking for homework. If a student had the homework, she complimented them on a good job. If not, she paddled him or her. She didn't exclude the girls, which a lot of teachers would have done.

By the time she got close to me, half the class was crying. I was beginning to panic, because I didn't have my homework. In just few minutes, I would be getting a paddling. She is now on my row. Then, too quickly, it's my turn.

"Jimmy, where is your homework?"

"I did mine, Ms. Talley, but I left it at home." There was a moment of silence, except for all those cry babies carrying on in the class.

"You really did your homework?"

"Yes, M'am, I did."

"Well, get up, go to your house, and bring it back."

I was stunned. I got up and went to the door, waiting on her to call me back. She didn't. I walked down the walkway going away from her class toward home. I just knew she would call me back any second. She didn't.

I am now at the street we lived on. I stood on the corner for a while, trying to figure out what to do next. The way I saw it, I had two choices. The first is to go home where I have no math homework waiting for me. If I went home and my mom was there, I could get killed. That choice didn't make much sense to me. The second choice was to go back to school, confess my sin, and take a paddling. Maybe there was a third choice. Maybe I could lie again.

I went with the third choice. When I walked back into the class, the other students' wailing was down to a few sniffles.

"Where is your homework, Jimmy," Ms. Talley asked.

"When I got home the doors were locked and no one was home."

She asked me again where my homework was. I think she was fishing for the truth, but my answer was the same. "I couldn't get in the house to get it."

"Then you'll have to stay in at recess and do the homework again. Then tomorrow, you bring the copy you left at home and put it on my desk as soon as you get here."

"Yes, M'am." I was one happy little liar.

Life was good.

THE MISSING DOLLAR

At the time of this story, I am in the third grade in Homerville Elementary School. My teacher was Ms. Whatley. She lived one street over from our home. Her two children, Patsy and Steve, were both a little older than me, but I would occasionally play at their home after school.

Steve was a good pole vaulter, and Patsy was very good at basketball. I think Steve was close to the best in the state in pole vaulting his senior year. The Whatleys had a saw dust pit in their back yard, and many times I watched Steve go over the top of the bar at ten feet. His senior year, he set the school record with a vault well over twelve feet. That was pretty darned high, especially when you're a third-grader looking up at that bar.

Later, when I was a teenager, I tried some vaults, but my best try was about six feet. I didn't like the fall after the vault. It was not my sport, but I loved to watch Steve go up and over, and then move the bar up for a new high mark.

I am certain that Ms. Whatley was the tallest teacher I ever had. When I was in the third grade, she looked about seven feet tall or taller. When she spoke, we listened, because the woman was all business. My behavior in her class was the best of my school career.

This story took place on a normal Monday. The first thing we did when school started each week was to go to Ms. Whatley's desk, row by row, to pay our lunch money and get a ticket. The lunch tickets cost one dollar for a week. I was seated in about the third row in the middle of the class. Our row went up, and as we stood in line waiting to pay, I was talking with a classmate right before it was my turn to pay.

I paid my dollar, got my ticket, and went back to my seat. All the other rows paid and got their tickets, so everything was normal and calm.

Shortly after we were all seated again, Ms. Whatley's daughter, Patsy, comes into the room to get her lunch money from her mother. Ms. Whatley had placed Patsy's dollar on the desk for her, prior to us paying for our lunches, but now the dollar was gone. Our teacher lost her temper and was some kind of mad. She then started accusing one of us of getting the dollar. I am thinking, *I'm so happy it's not me.* She had blood in her eyes, and I'm certain that if she found out who took the dollar, some form of torture awaited the poor soul.

She went on about the dollar for a while, but no one made a move to give it back. We were young, but we were not fools. All we knew was that whoever did this awful deed, their lives would never be the same. Then, Ms. Whatley calmed down to take a different approach.

"Whoever took the dollar may have done it accidently. Yes, that's what I think probably happened." We did not have thieves back in those days, not in the third grade, anyway.

"I want each of you to stand beside your desk," Ms. Whatley said. I'm thinking that a body search is in the making. "Boys, check your front pockets to see if you have a dollar there." As I felt in my pocket, I was relieved not to find a dollar. "Now, check your back pockets." Ok, I can do that, too. As soon as I put my hand in my back left pocket, guess what I found. OH NO! I paid for my lunch ticket with her dollar and still had mine.

I almost died right there on the spot. So, now what do I do? Due to an extreme case of fear, I sat back down at my desk without a confession, and a dollar bill in my pocket that was not mine. It was my teacher's money. When no one confessed to the crime, Ms. Whatley said that during recess she would go to the teacher's lounge, and whoever had the dollar could put it back on her desk and no one would ever know.

It is now recess, and I have a decision to make. First of all, I figured, she didn't do a body search, and I'm safely out of the room. I'm feeling better now, but I'm still not out of the woods. I could take the money back, keep it and be rich for a day, or get rid of it. I thought about what a dollar would buy. I could go to Harper's Drugstore after school to get a cherry coke and several new comic books. Hmmm. What would you do? I didn't trust her about going to the teacher's lounge. I was thinking that she would be hiding under her desk, and if I took it back to the desk, she would jump out – "Gotcha!"

I went with plan three: get rid of it. We had trash bins on the playground where each day the trash was burned. This was before the EPA started breathing down our necks. I eased over to a trash can and looked around casually. I placed the dollar about half way down and left the area. I didn't do the right thing, but I lived. Guess you could say I had money to burn.

I am certain now, many years later, that Ms. Whatley wouldn't have killed me, but I didn't know that back then. Her daughter Patsy is a Facebook friend of mine, and she will soon read this story. Patsy, can I mail you a dollar and call it even? I hope you were able to eat that week. Sorry. Please forgive me

HAPPY DAYS

Here's what we did back in the days when I was growing up. I've seen lists like this one on Facebook and just had to throw in my two cents worth.

Playing with your toy cars and trucks under a house was so fun. Most houses in our neighborhood were built well off the ground, and it was dirty and cool under them. We were so small and the beams were so high that we never bumped our heads. You could easily identify the kids who either played under houses or shot a lot of marbles by the knee holes in their blue jeans.

Going to a traveling tent movie at the cost of one nickel.

Getting to see a real live medicine show in Homerville.

Skating at the once-a-year portable skating rink with a tent roof. They strung chicken wire around the outside to keep us in, but it didn't always work.

Playing marbles and going home with more than I came with.

Beating the girls in a game of hopscotch was always a thriller.

Going to the movie for a dollar and change. That amount included your date and drinks and popcorn for two. After the movie for a dollar more, you got two hamburgers, two fries, and two drinks at Clyde's drive-in restaurant on the Fargo highway. Clyde's was the best for awesome food and service.

Going to the A&W Drive-in restaurant in Waycross for a foot-long hot dog and a large root beer.

Paying only 19 cents per gallon for gas.

Buying a large oatmeal cookie with a Dr. Pepper for eleven cents at the store.

Buying a block of ice at the Talley Ice Company and watching it get made into crushed ice.

Getting your shoes repaired at the shoe shop. We didn't get new shoes very often, so the repairman had good job security.

Having a silver dollar in your pocket.

Life was good.

NOT SO HAPPY DAYS

You have some of my happy memories from childhood, so it's only fair that you listen to some of the bad memories, too. The good far outweighed the bad, but not every day was sunshine and ballgames.

Every summer my mom would drop me off at the county health department on a Saturday morning to get shots for the next school year. Being the nice guy I was, I always let the other kids break line ahead of me. I could keep that up for three hours, just standing around and talking to everyone.

Then, just before they closed the office for lunch, Mrs. Chauncey, the nurse, and her helper would grab me and drag me up for my turn. I put up a good fight and did a lot of screaming and crying, but the women won out. I hated those shots.

Another bad memory from my childhood involved getting into fights with a group of boys in my sixth grade class. After each fight, we got a paddling that was well-deserved. The worst part was that we all had to go to the principal's office for the morning, lunch, and afternoon recesses. We also had to write "I will not fight" one thousand times on paper.

It was a week before we all saw another recess. Whatever happened to letting the punishment fit the crime? Don't you think all of that was excessive punishment for one little fight that mostly consisted of us daring each other to step over some line or to take the first swing? Maybe the punishment was stiff, because we were habitual offenders.

Do you have any bad Christmas memories? No, you were probably the good little kid that Santa loaded up with stuff every year.

When my friends and I were in the second grade, the first day back in school after Christmas, the teacher asked each student to tell something Santa brought them. Thank the Lord, we all got something that year. The list ranged from fruit to bicycles.

It was all going good until it was Martha Carswell's turn. She got a horse. A horse, she said with pride. And it wasn't that kind of pride that makes you comb your hair and gargle in the morning so you're presentable. No, it was that kind of pride that made everyone else want to puke.

A horse was the dream of everyone in our class, boys and girls alike. We all wanted to be cowboys and cowgirls: Roy Rogers and Dale Evans. Wow, how did Santa pull that off? And why Martha? Why not some little boy who had to get shots at the health department every summer? It didn't seem right to me.

One year as Christmas approached, I was staying with my Uncle J.H. and Aunt Deloris in Thomasville. They had three girls I would play with: Janice, the oldest and just a year younger than me, Rhonda, and Beth. We all played well together, so I'm not even sure how this one came about.

We were out in the backyard and a discussion came up about Santa Claus. I quickly informed Janice that there was no Santa Claus: Big time mistake on my part. Janice starts crying and running to her mom, shouting, "There's no Santa Claus." In less than a minute, Aunt Deloris and I were having "a talk." You know the kind, where the kid doesn't do much talking, and then gets a beating. And then the adult calls your mom to come get you.

After "the talk" with Aunt Deloris, I once again believed in jolly old Saint Nick. Never let anyone tell you there's not a Santa Claus.

When I was a kid most families had freezers where we could put up vegetables from the garden or deer meat. In those days, the freezer manufacturers weren't too concerned about their customers' safety, so they didn't bother to hook up a ground wire. Now, when you buy an appliance, it's grounded. Let's all say amen!

I will never forget the freezer we had sitting on our concrete carport. If you ever touched it when you were barefooted, it would knock the crap out of you. Since I went barefoot most of the time, I always got shocked when I touched the freezer, each time vowing never to do that again.

The day finally came when I was able to keep my vow. I was barefooted and grabbed the door to open the freezer and ZAP! I took a full load of electricity that knocked me to the concrete floor. I don't have it on video, but I imagine myself, laying there and shaking all over for about two or three minutes. Never again.

The meat freezers at the grocery stores weren't grounded then either. I recall getting shocked many times at a store named Chauncey's Meats in Homerville. Keith Chauncey was the store owner's son, and he worked for his dad after school and in the summers. Keith was a few years older than me, and he was as mean as they come.

I think he lived for the moment when a kid came into the store barefooted, because then he could think of a way to get them to touch the meat counter. He would just die laughing when we got zapped. It's hard to believe that Keith turned out to be a preacher, and a darned good one.

When I was in high school, one of my favorite classes was Shop. Mr. Brooks was very smart and a great teacher. He taught me a lot about small engines, welding, and forestry.

The school had two places off campus where we would go to learn about real world subjects, hands on. One was forestry. We actually had a small forested area that we kept up. One of the things I enjoyed learning was how to get a log and truss it up to the top rack of the pulpwood trailer.

The other area off campus was a hog operation, and it was messy and fun. We had to be careful not to mess up our clothes as we did the work that Mr. Brooks told us to do, particularly on the day he taught us how to castrate a hog. He was going to tell us what to do, but we had to do it.

My hog mates were Stanley Lankford and W.C. Fender. We got the poor pig cornered and did what Mr. Brooks told us to do. He said this was good for the pig, but I don't think Porky agreed. Then Mr. Brooks told us that the hog would get larger and make more money on the market. Oh, so it wasn't exactly going to work out for the hog's good.

When we finished the unpleasant work and turned the hog loose, W.C. said, "See you tomorrow, Lucky."

On the unpleasant memories I've shared with you in this story, that's how I felt some days.

No Dog Night

Back in the 1960s a county or regional fair was a big deal, above any earthly place we local Homerville kids could hope to go. At age twelve, when I was invited to go to one, you'd have thought I died and went to heaven.

My best friend for the week, Danny Ray, and his parents asked me if I wanted to go with them to the regional fair in Waycross. Heck, yeah! Are you kidding me? I ran home to beg my mother to let me go, and not only did she say yes, she reached in her purse and pulled out Abe Lincoln: five dollars! Life is good.

The Smiths drive us over to Waycross, and Danny Ray and I are about to wet our pants with anticipation. Uncle Haskell, as I called him, parks the car, and the fairgrounds are buzzing with excitement: multi-colored lights, people everywhere, rides slinging kids around, music, and five bucks in my hot little pocket. WAHOO!

Uncle Haskell buys our tickets, and we are in. Before you can get to the amusement park and rides, everyone had to go through a maze lined with prize-winning jelly, pies, cakes, hogs, goats, chickens, and rabbits. After about five minutes of oohing and aahing over the winners' triumphs, we came to the end of the maze and walked through a big gate that opened onto the amusement park.

To my twelve-year-old eyes, the scene was like a new day breaking, and I could hear angels singing: AAAHHH, OOOHHH,

AAAAAAHHHHHH! Lights, rides, people, games, and me with five big ones: Heaven.

Right in front of me, a man called for my attention. "Hey, kid, come here. I want to show you something." The Smiths were busy looking around and Danny Ray took off for something that had caught his eye, so I went over to see what the man had. Behind him on a big board were all kinds of prizes.

"See these prizes, kid? I want to give you one. Which one do you want?"

I looked them over, all kinds of stuffed animals, and pointed at a big, blonde fluffy dog.

"Okay, the dog. Give me a quarter, and all you have to do is throw these three balls in that basket. Do that, and the dog is yours. You can throw three balls in a basket, can't you boy?"

Humph, are you kidding me? Sounds like a deal, I'm thinking. He even shows me how. One, two, three – his balls go right in. He lets me have a warm-up toss, and it sails in: sure thing. Heck, what's a quarter when you have five bucks? On my first attempt, I got two of the three balls in the basket.

"That's good, kid. Not many people get two out of three on their first try. Give me another quarter, and if you get all three balls in this time, I'll give you the dog and your money back."

Who could say no to that great opportunity? Fast forward the story five minutes, and the guy has all my money. I didn't even have money for a Coke and a corn dog, much less that big, stuffed dog. I spent the rest of the night wandering around the fair, watching Danny Ray wave at me as he passed by on the next ride he was on. Darn him.

It was a sad night for a twelve-year-old, but I learned a valuable lesson or two: First, no Las Vegas for me in the future. If a guy at a little country fair could take five dollars from me in five minutes, imagine what they could get out of me in Sin City.

Second, if I ever wanted a stuffed dog again, I would save my hard-earned money and buy one. There's no such thing as a sure thing. Pay cash.

WHAT A DAY

Many years back in my early teens, my good friend and neighbor Danny Ray had a skip-the-school-day plan. The plan worked many times, but came to an end a few weeks after it started. I almost skipped school with him that day, but backed out at the last moment. Looking back, I'm glad I did.

This is how it all went down. Danny Ray would wait for his parents to leave for work. Then he and any fellow school-skipping friends would hang around the house to watch TV and to play. What a great life.

The only problem with the plan was that his parents would come home for a short lunch break, and then head back to work. During this time, Danny Ray and Company would climb an outside ladder that leaned up next to the ceiling entrance door. They would climb into the attic during his parents' lunch break. When the adults went back to work, the boys would come back down to enjoy the good life.

On the day the plan ended, another of our neighbors, Mike Davis, was Danny Ray's accomplice. This day was Mike's first time to participate in the skip-school program. Life is really good when you have a friend to share life with and you're getting away with something.

The morning went great, and now Danny Ray and Mike are in the attic, sitting on the rafters while the parents are eating lunch. For some reason Mike decided to move to a different rafter. I'm sure it was tough to sit on one rafter for a long period of time.

As Mike moved, he stepped wrong and fell through the sheetrock ceiling. Where do you think he fell as he went down into the house? If you had said the Smith's enamel kitchen table, you would have been right.

Uncle Haskell and Aunt Lucille thought the world had come to an end. As soon as Mike hit the table, he was off and running out the front door to his house. Three scared folks in one house at one time is a rare event.

As Uncle Haskell recovered, Danny Ray came in the back door, pretending to wonder what happened. Uncle Haskell knew his son well enough to know that he was involved somehow, so he went ahead and applied one good tail whipping. Danny Ray only skipped school one more time after that incident.

The other time Danny Ray skipped school, he and a few friends skipped sixth period. As they were leaving school, Danny Ray ran a stop sign and was broad-sided. The wreck almost totaled his pretty blue 1960 Chevy truck. Everyone was uninjured, but Uncle Haskell told Danny Ray that he wasn't going to repair the vehicle. It stayed in the Smith's yard a few months until Danny Ray finally got it going again. I remember it was the only dented-up truck in town with no front windshield. It was very cold to ride in during the winter, but great to hunt out of.

All the boys in our neighborhood learned a lot from Danny Ray's mistakes.

TENTH GRADE BLUES

The ninth grade ended up being one of the best years of my life: Good grades, football, no paddlings, hanging around with older kids, and freedom from Mr. Mims, our old junior high principal and warden.

During the summer break after my ninth grade year, someone told me that the high school in Homerville was getting a new principal. Guess who? Yes, Mr. Lloyd D. Mims. I am thinking, *my school life is over.* Three years of torture lie ahead. Sure enough, he did get the job, and the good news, if there was any, was that he knew my name.

His first day, he started tough and explained the rules to all students, plus a few new ones added since his days in Dupont. Boys and girls could not hold hands on campus. That was a new one. I agreed with that one, though.

Mr. Mims was a big supporter of our ball teams and all school events. Often I would see him at football practice, and he would always speak and ask how I was doing. In high school I saw a different side of him, a caring side, but he never slacked off on his rules. I would rate him pretty high on the list of people who helped me move up in life.

In 1968 I graduated from high school and was off to college at Abraham Baldwin Agricultural College (ABAC) in Tifton and later, Georgia Southern at Statesboro, Georgia. When I came home, I would occasionally see Mr. Mims, and he would always take time to chat with me. He later went to Valdosta High School as principal during the time I was attending college.

I guess the biggest surprise of my life occurred as I was finishing at Georgia Southern. I got a call from Mr. Mims. He wanted to know how I was doing, and then he said he had someone who wanted to talk with me. On the other end of the phone was a shocker. I am now talking with Coach Wight Bazemore: Mr. Valdosta, Mr. Football, The Man!

Coach Bazemore said, "Mr. Mims has told me lots of good things about you, and I want to offer you a job as one of my junior high football coaches."

Of course, I was in shock, and I told them I would get back in touch with them. Wow, a chance to work with Coach Bazemore. Of all people, me!

It could have been a life-changer, and I am certain it would have been a great journey. When I called them back, I told them I had decided to stay in the Statesboro area. I coached for one year in Effingham County before going the route of working in various management jobs for the next twenty-six years.

Occasionally I think about that phone conversation. Many times I have wondered what might have been if I had decided to coach with the great Wight Bazemore. I'm still humbled by the job offer from those two great men. Thanks, Mr. Mims, for the chance.

BIKES AND GIRLS

I was invited to a party across town at a classmate's home. I was going into the ninth grade, and it was during the summer. I loved my bike, a red and white Western Flier with a basket and a big seat.

I know things have to be screwed up in our country nowadays. Have you noticed the bikes people are riding? There are 10 speeds, upside down handlebars, and seats so slim and hard that most folks need a "Caution, Overload" butt sign on back of the bike. To top things off, the manufacturers now save money by substituting one-inch tires for the old, steady two-inchers.

At the time some of my friends were getting new cars like Mustangs, VW bugs, or an older car or truck, I was fully content with my bike. I was the last person my age to ditch old faithful, and that was a sad day in my life.

When I went to the party that day, I was the only one who rode a bike. Everyone else either drove a car or caught a ride with someone who had one. Over the next several months, I went to many get-togethers at the same home. It finally dawned on me that these were planned pairing parties. The host was playing matchmaker, and the number of boys and girls invited was always even, a boy for each girl.

At those parties we had Coke and chips and listened to Beatle songs on the record player. "I Want to Hold Your Hand" was played pretty often, so I guess that should have tipped me off as to what was going on.

After refreshments the lights in the small room dimmed, and the girls grabbed a guy. I was picked by a girl I didn't know, and she said, "Let's sit in this chair together." I'm thinking this is not cool, because she was kind of heavy, but I gave it a try. I was the first to leave at 8:30, telling her I had a nine o'clock curfew. That could have been the truth.

As the summer passed, I sold my bike for $10 and started walking to the parties, to school, and anywhere else I needed to go. Once I made my destination, I would later either walk back home or catch a ride from a friend. I guess this was my first step of going from boyhood to manhood, or teenhood would be a better description.

I still miss my old Western Flier, but now that I'm older, I have a new bike. Getting old is great.

Life is good.

DANCING

I think my generation grew up in one of the best times since the world was created. It was the best, but it was also a time of big changes for our culture that would affect future generations. It's hard to believe now, but many kids I grew up with couldn't go to a movie or a dance, and their parents wouldn't allow the devil-box, TV, in their homes. I was allowed to go to movies and dances if I had the money, and we had a TV at our house. Maybe that's the reason I turned out far from perfect: too many movies, too much dancing, and way too much TV.

Most kids my age loved Friday nights after the football games. Every town had live band dances, either on Friday or Saturday nights or both. No drugs or excessive alcohol was in sight. It was just good clean fun.

The top local band in our area was The Wanderers. I still recall most of the band members: Keith Chauncey, Wallace Colley, Mickey Allen, Mira Barrett, Ronnie Smith, Andy Kemp, Mike Henderson, and Freddy Landrum. Those guys were great. Of course, they were not all in the band at the same time. Their best songs were "Shout" and "We Got to Go".

If you could travel to Tifton, Waycross, or Valdosta, you could listen to a headline band for a few dollars. To name a few, there were Percy Sledge, The Tams, The Lettermen, The Swingin' Medallions, and The Box Tops. They would be right on the floor with you as they played and sang.

I ended up being a pretty good dancer. Prior to going to my first dance in the ninth grade, I took dance lessons. The lessons were at my house with my friend, Orrin Deason, and our home radio. Orrin and I were the students and the dance instructors. When a song came on the air, we practiced in my mom's kitchen. We made sure no one was home, and we never told anyone what we were doing.

We practiced with a broom when a slow song came on. It cracks me up to think about it now, but we did what we had to do to learn to dance. We did it, and as The Tams used to sing, it was a good time to "Be Young, Be Foolish, Be Happy"!

WHY I LOVE ALGEBRA

The year is 1965. It is my first day of high school in Homerville. It is the place to be. The story begins in my fifth period Algebra class. Our teacher was Coach Robbins, who was also my football coach.

One day I got to class and took a seat near the back of the class. Right before the tardy bell rang, three senior girls came in. They were three of the prettiest girls I had seen in my life, and I was in class with them. Life is good.

I had first seen these girls at football games when I was in junior high school. They were stars at the games, even more than the players, because they were majorettes. Even when I was one of the kids running wild under the bleachers during the games, I had noticed them. I had never expected to meet them, much less to be in a class with them.

At this point I didn't think things could get any better, but they did. Since I was almost late getting to class and they were, too, the girls ended up sitting near me. Carmen sat at the desk next to me. Anna was in the next row, and Martha Jon was right behind her.

As I sat there, it was like being frozen in time. I thought about a movie named 10 about the perfect girl, but I had a perfect 30 within a few feet of me. I was glued to my chair, and when Coach Robbins started talking about Algebra, I focused my thoughts on him and away from my situation, as much as I could.

The next day was a life changer, maybe for all of us. I was back in class surrounded by all that beauty and paying attention to Coach Robbins, when out of the blue, Carmen touched my shoulder. Wow, she touched me. Then I felt her breath on my neck and heard a soft whisper from her. She asked me if I understood this crap. That's close to the word she used, anyway. My response was yes, I did. Am I digging myself a hole? Maybe!

Coach Robbins said he would give us a test each Friday, so Carmen's plan was for me to slide to the left, so she could copy my paper. I would change a few I had from the right answer to the wrong one, so our test papers did not look alike. She would let Anna see her page, and then it would filter back to Martha Jon.

The plan worked for a year, and they all finished with A's in Algebra. I can't remember what I finished with, either an A or a B. My mission was to help them, not me. I had to make less for the team. One key point: By asking me to help them, Carmen motivated me to study Algebra and do my homework. In theory, I hoped to be ready for them to make 100 on each Friday test. Algebra was my love.

What is cool is that all three of these ladies were friends with me for a long time after high school, and all three ended up being great teachers. Yes, teachers. I guess I did my part to help make this a better world, one Algebra problem at a time.

MY SPORTING LIFE

THE BASKETBALL CHAMP

The boys in Homerville loved to go to Linda James' house after school for three very good reasons: her house was centrally located in our neighborhood, the James home had a great big yard for the kids to play in, and darn, Linda was pretty. We played catch, kick the can, and basketball. Did I say basketball? Every day we played basketball.

When we got to her house, Linda would be outside at her goal, shooting. The boys would show up one by one until we had two teams. The players were Linda, Danny Ray, Wink, Mike, and me. Linda would always let one of us decide who we wanted on our team. She would take the leftovers, and then the game was on.

It was three on two, and Linda's team was her and the leftover boy. We would play for an hour or so, and Linda and her teammate always won. She could dribble, pass, and shoot, and seldom did she ever miss.

Once in high school Wink and Linda were both on the varsity boys and girls teams. Practice paid off for those two. The rest of us paid to watch them play. It was twenty-five cents per game, but you would get your money's worth. We could go to two games in the old green, wooden barn gym, and to see Linda shooting from all over the court, seldom missing, was one thing that made life good.

In high school, Linda once scored over forty points in a single game, and there were no three-pointers back then. She was the best, and I wish she had been on the boy's team for the second game each evening. I'm certain she would have been All-American in college, but at the time, colleges in our part of the country didn't have girl basketball teams.

Folks in Clinch County will never forget her ball-playing skills and her sweet personality. I still recall a comment she made to me once as we were leaving the Homerville movie theater. She had a date with another guy, and she said, "Jimmy, do you know who you favor?" I had no clue. She said, "Steve McQueen, the cowboy on the TV show, "Wanted: Dead or Alive". I was disappointed when I went home, looked in the mirror for my actor's good looks, and realized she was just being kind.

Linda was a great person, and it was an honor to have played neighborhood basketball with her and to have counted her as a friend.

THE 1968 CLINCH
COUNTY PANTHERS

In my senior year of high school, I was lucky enough to be a part of the football team. You might not think I was very lucky when I tell you that we started off the season by losing our first six games. We did have a good team, but our record didn't indicate it.

After those six losses, the coaches decided to change quarterbacks, and after that, we rolled, winning our next four games. The last game of the season we even beat Berrien County and that was the first time our school had ever beaten them. We were a class B school, and they were in A classification, one up from us. I think if we could have started the season over, we would have been state champs.

The seniors on that team were John Barrett, Orrin Deason, Corky Ingram, Curtis Hughes, Harry Hughes, Gary Morrison, and me. Those guys were the best, and they still are. Ok, so you're thinking, *Where is the story here?* I'll think a little deeper and try to find one. For sure, there is one.

1968 was the first year of integration at our school. It was no big deal. I never knew of any problems with the new black students. That same year, Clinch County High School also got about forty new students from, of all places, Manor, Georgia. You pronounce the name of the town like, "Mainer". Now that was trouble.

Manor was across the county line in Ware County. In 1968 the Ware County Board of Education voted to close the school in the little crossroads town. Since Manor was closer to Homerville than to Waycross, an arrangement was made for their students to attend our school. The first thing their boys did was to try to take our girlfriends away from us.

Once we got that deal straightened out, they turned out to be a great group of kids. Over time a bond formed, and Homerville came to love Manor and they loved us. To heck with Ware County, we all thought.

During our first week of football practice back home, after a week of summer camp down in Fargo, Coach Robbins gathered us up and told us we would have a new player on the team the next day. His name was Henry Davis, one of the first black students to attend our high school. Coach Robbins said that Henry had never played football, but he wanted to. Very interesting, we thought.

We players were thinking, No big deal. We need all the help we can get. But, we did have a Henry Davis Plan. It was the same plan we used to break in freshmen and other new players. Though it was a non-coach-approved plan, we all had gone through it. I recall my first day on the football team when it happened to me, but that's another story.

The plan was to call plays on offense that would be directed toward Henry. For example, the quarterback would call, "Henry Davis Interception". Then, with Henry on the defense, the quarterback would throw the ball right at him. For the first few weeks, Henry would drop the ball every time. Darn! He was supposed to catch it, so three or four guys could hit him and break him into the Panther Power Club.

I still remember the day he managed to hang onto the ball. Several of us hit him hard, but Henry jumped up from the pile with the ball, and he was super happy. He did a little dance, and the coaches complimented him on a good job. Darn! That wasn't in the plan.

When Henry was on offense, he was a running back. The linemen would let the defense know when he was getting the ball and which hole he would be running to. We were ready to make a believer out of him, so when he ran to the appointed place, eight or nine of us smacked him good. When he finally got out from under the pile, he looked like the happiest kid ever. Henry couldn't wait to get the ball again.

You have to admire a guy like that. Week three into the season, Henry was just one of the 24 Panthers on the 1968 team. He was a friend to all of us, and integration was just something the adults would have to worry about.

MY FIRST SPRING FOOTBALL PRACTICE

I am now a 120 pound eighth-grader. The head football coach at the high school announces that any of us who want to be on the varsity team the next year will need to participate in spring practice. Of course, I signed up, because my dream was to play varsity football at Clinch County High School.

We are now in pads, and the seniors are trying their best to kill us younger players. They appear to love it. The coaches don't seem to mind. I suppose it was their way of saying, "Welcome to the team." It didn't seem like a welcome party to us eighth-graders.

I will never forget my first day when the coach told me to go in and play safety during the scrimmage. I am now on the field, looking fearfully at the first string giants on the other side of the ball. These new seniors and graduating seniors were heroes of mine the year before, and now here I am on the field with them. Is life good or bad, I'm thinking? I would soon find out.

Most plays seemed directed at me. I was first hit on each play by Allen Kennedy, a 145 pound senior. Next was Jack Hart, a graduating senior who was 6'6" and well over 200 pounds. Jack played college basketball later at South Georgia College and then at Valdosta State.

Then, I was expected to tackle Hal Peagler. He was a graduating senior who went to the University of Georgia as a player. Hal was big and fast, and he enjoyed running over me or anyone else that got between him and the goal line. After I was hit by Allen and Jack, Hal didn't have to worry much about me. Not once did I slow him down or tackle him, but I tried. I took all the licks, and somehow got up and tried again.

I think some folks in Homerville may still be talking about my highlight play of the practice. All day Allen would hit me, then Jack ran over me, and if I was still standing Hal finished me off on the way to another touchdown. Over and over this happened to me all day, until my little victory took place.

Allen got his hit on me and here came Jack. I'm not sure why, self-preservation probably, but on this one play, I lowered my helmet and waited for the impact. Boom, but I was still standing. Jack was now on the backside of me, out of breath and holding his privates. They tell me that the flip he turned over me was spectacular. Because of the size difference, it was the perfect spot for me to hit to take the giant down.

All the other guys on defense were high-fiving me, and the coaches were beside themselves. Jack finally got up and practice was called to an end. I kept my distance from Jack, because I thought he might try to kill me.

Life is good.

FARGO AND FOOTBALL

The first camp I ever attended was the Clinch County Varsity Football Camp at Fargo, Georgia. I went to camp there all four years I was in high school. I often wondered why we went to Fargo for camp. Why not go to Valdosta or Waycross? Looking back, it probably had something to do with avoiding distractions, because there weren't any girls around our camp at Fargo Elementary School.

Some of the highlights (lowlights?) of the camp included:

Running along highway 441 at daylight, one mile north and then one mile back to camp on the other side of the highway.

Practicing contact drills (hitting each other) from breakfast to lunch.

Showering outside with only cold water. Okay, maybe that was a highlight, because it was some kind of hot in August, and once you got used to the water, you didn't want to get out.

More contact drills (hitting each other) all afternoon. The only bad injury I saw during camp was when Charlie Robbins broke his collarbone. Actually, I don't think he broke it, but he was there at the time, and it looked like it hurt.

Our coaches always wanted us to be tough, even though they were almost killing us. I'm surprised we didn't lose a player or two to heat stroke. The coaches of that day didn't believe in drinking water during practice. We were in full pads, and the temperature was around 100 degrees most days. We could only drink water from the shower after practice, no water pails along the sideline.

Coach Griffis would say, "When the going gets tough, the tough get going." Whatever that meant!

I would often get what we called cotton mouth during practice, so one day I got the bright idea of trying to hide a small bottle of water in my pads. I got caught and had to run laps around the practice field. Death was close that day.

For fun we would play cards at night, usually some poker game. We played for chewing gum, and one year, I came home with ten packs of gum. We slept on cots in the elementary school lunch room with no fans and open windows. Did I mention mosquitoes? Fargo is close to the Okefenokee Swamp, and I wouldn't have been surprised to see some of those golly-whoppers toting off one of the small boys at night.

You won't believe my main football camp highlight. Are you ready? My freshman year we had a volunteer coach come to help the team get ready for the season. He was a really good coach, but he had one big problem: hemorrhoids.

At night he would warm up a pot of hot water in one of the big lunchroom cooking pots and sink his behind in it for a little relief. Quite a sight! Years later it dawned on me that we would eat beans out of that pot the next day.

When camp was over, we rode the school bus back to Homerville, in theory ready for our first game the next Friday night. We never won an opening game when I was in high school. I am a firm believer that we were still so tired and beat up from camp that we didn't have anything left for the real game.

Thank you, good Lord, for watching over us.

Canoeing the Okefenokee

As a kid I loved growing up near the Okefenokee Swamp and the Suwannee River. Both places were magnificent, full of beauty and life on a large scale, but at the same time you would feel as if you owned them. I've been on the river and in the swamp for hours without seeing another person. In every direction I looked, I saw a perfect picture of nature.

Even as I grew older, I still loved to go to the river and the swamp every chance I had. If you've never been and get the opportunity, please take it.

I had one unforgettable overnight camping trip in the Okefenokee. I had talked a group of co-workers into canoeing the swamp and spending the night out in it. All we needed was a permit to spend the night on one of the islands in the swamp, a few supplies, and five canoes for the ten of us. We made our plans, got the permit, and a month later, in June, we were launching our canoes. We were a happy group of campers...at that point.

We left from Stephen Foster State Park at the Fargo entrance, reached Billy's Lake, and turned left headed for our island. The skies were perfectly clear and a light breeze kept us cool. All around us we enjoyed cypress trees, water lilies, an occasional gator, and a big variety of birds.

Going to the island where we would spend the night, we were paddling with the current downstream. At times we would paddle down some side water ways that were only a few feet wide. Later we had to get out and pull our canoes over logs that had the way blocked. That part was not much fun.

The island was about eight miles from the State Park, and it took us until about six o'clock to get there. It wasn't exactly what we had pictured. It was just a small clearing on a ridge sticking out of the water. Our agenda was to set up our tents, cook a good meal over the hot coals of a campfire, and then sit around shooting the bull.

Nature has a way of changing plans. As we got the fire going, a major lightning and rain storm blew in and settled over us. It was bad, really bad. We scrambled to our tents right before dark set in. My roommate for the night was Robert Stump who was a veteran camper. This trip was one of my first camp outs.

The two of us shared a pup tent that was about five feet wide and three feet tall. I watched enviously as Robert put down a sheet of plastic on the ground, topped by a blow-up mattress and then his sleeping bag. He brought out a sheet to go over the sleeping bag, and, of course, he had a pillow and pillow case.

I rolled out my sleeping bag on the cold, hard ground.

Soon after dark, the rain started, and it was a toad-choker. It didn't take any time for my sleeping bag to get soaking wet, and I had nowhere to go. I lay there trying to will the rain to slack off, thinking that this is about as bad as it gets.

Then the coons showed up. There were so many of them it looked like a walking dead movie out there. I kept yelling and waving at them, trying to get the little bandits to move on. It was miserable; maybe worse than miserable.

Then I had to use the bathroom. I thought about battling the coons and dodging the lightning to get away from the tent, but it didn't seem worth the risk. Besides, Robert was cozy and snoring up on his air mattress, so he'd never know. I got as close to the front of the tent as I could without encountering coons, hunkered down to the three foot height of the tent, and let it fly into the dark. It would be washed away in seconds anyway. I was miserable; maybe worse than miserable.

I never got as much as a wink of sleep all night, but darned Robert did. I hated him at that moment. The minute he had laid down and pulled the sheet over him, his head rested on the softest pillow in the world covered by one of those pillow cases with the faint fragrance of laundry detergent on it, and he was sound asleep. Robert slept all night, darn his soul. Misery wants company, but I had none. I lived through that miserable, wet, coon-filled night, but just barely.

Later in life, I took my family on many camping trips. I remember one in particular, a week's stay in Deep Creek Campgrounds near Cherokee, North Carolina. I slept like a dead coon in a huge tent on an air-filled mattress, comfy with my sheets, down-filled pillow, fragrant pillow case, and an electric fan cooling my dry, dream-filled body. Yes, we had electricity in our tent! Aaahhhh!

FISHING

I will never forget one Sunday when we came home from church in Hazlehurst. We were eating lunch, and I asked my son, Jay, what he had learned in Sunday School that morning. He was about seven years old at the time.

He said they had learned about Jesus going fishing and what a great fisherman the Lord was. "Daddy," Jay said, "Jesus went fishing one time, and they caught so many fish, the boat started sinking."

Jay went on to add a lot of detail about who was fishing and where they were, so I was impressed with how well he had listened to the Sunday School lesson. I told him that I was proud of him and thanked him for sharing the story.

At that point, I thought Jay was finished with the story, but he was still thinking about it and how the story of Jesus fishing applied to our lives today.

"Daddy, why don't you take Jesus fishing with you sometime? When you go, you never catch anything." He was right.

The moral to this story still lingers in my head. Why don't we take Jesus with us everywhere we go? If we want to be successful at whatever we do, we need his power and guidance every day. The next time I go fishing, I'll take Jesus with me.

How about you: To take or not to take, that's the question.

NOT ROBIN HOOD

Many years back I decided to buy a bow and start hunting deer during archery season. I bought my bow on the Monday before deer season was to start on the next Saturday. A week of practice in the back yard should be ample time to hone my skill and kill a deer the first day of the season.

That Monday I went to the back of the Piggly Wiggly Grocery store in Hazlehurst, Georgia and came away with a cardboard box from their trash bin for my target. My box was not just any box; it was a Tide box, maybe two by three feet in size. It was about the basic size of a deer's torso, so I had the right idea.

My goal was to be able to hit the T in Tide by Friday afternoon. My second goal was to kill a deer on my first hunting trip that golden Friday.

That Monday afternoon I shot arrows all over our back yard and that of our neighbor, never coming close to the box, much less the T. The box was safe. The neighbors were not. Tuesday was a new day, however, and I hit the box on occasion, rare occasion.

As the week progressed, though, I was able to hit not only the box, but every once in a while, the sacred T. By Thursday, I was hitting the T in Tide often, even from 30 yards away. I was good. It just took me some time to learn how to use the sight pins on the bow and to estimate distance accurately. Looking back, it was easy for me to become a pro in one week, due to my commitment.

On Saturday, I am not anxious for the early morning alarm to sound, but when it does, I'm up and out the door in no time.

At this point, I am hunting a river swamp area, hoping to see a deer and to score a kill. About 9:30, I heard a sound behind me, and I glanced back to spot a large doe thirty yards away, standing broadside, a textbook shot. This is going to be easy.

I choose the 30 yard pin. I take a deep breath, pull the arrow back as in practice and think of shooting the T in Tide. I release the arrow and, darn, I miss. The arrow goes over the doe's back by one inch. She stops feeding, looks at where the arrow has gone, and strolls closer to me.

The deer is now 25 yards from me. I ease the second arrow into place, make mental adjustments, and select the 25 yard pin. Easy kill, I'm thinking. No way I can miss again. I aim and release the arrow. Darn, it goes under the doe's stomach by an inch.

So, the deer again moves toward me. She's now 20 yards away. I select the 20 yard pin and make more mental adjustments. I am now thinking, *This deer is a goner.* If I can hit the T in Tide almost every shot, how could I miss a 20 yard shot? Deep breath, aim, release the arrow, and you guessed it: I miss again, in front of the deer's neck by... one inch.

What the heck is going on? This cannot be happening. I'm missing by no more that one inch each time. This deer is doing everything except screaming, "Kill me, kill me, you fool!" I have two arrows left. The deer saunters up another 5 yards, now only 15 yards from me.

Mental adjustments, 15 yard pin, deep breath, aim arrow, release: miss again by no more than an inch. This is a true story. I promise you. Why would a man tell this on himself if it weren't true? This time the arrow goes right by the deer's rear. Wow, this is unreal.

Still, the doe doesn't run away. Why should she? The deer is now standing so far under me that she has to tilt her head back to see me. I place my last arrow into the bow, my knees knocking. The deer walks slowly away, and I can't even raise the bow to take a shot. I just stood there and watched her disappear into the woods.

This deer was one of many that got away from me over the years. Good for them. I later got a gravity-based sight system and became a much better archer, but on other hunts, I just could not bring myself to shoot a deer. I enjoyed watching them, thinking, Steak is better than venison any day.

Glad I missed.

My Working Life

TOBACCO FIELDS

I was around thirteen years old when I started working in the tobacco fields during the summer. My first summer I made one hundred dollars, and I saved it all until school started. I made three dollars per day, so this money represented lots of hours and days of hard work.

We worked from day light till dark. Even though it was hot and hard, it was one of the best things that ever happened to me: a job and the benefits of working. That job was a stepping stone to learning skills that I'm certain prepared me for better jobs as I grew older. Plus, I got a great reward each day of three dollars, cash money. I used the money to buy school clothes, pay school fees, and to buy lunch. It lasted me until football season was over, and then I would find other part time jobs for the remainder of the school term.

Our day started before dawn when Ms. Young, an older neighbor, would pick up the workers. She drove us out to the Nobles Farm on the Fargo highway. We took our own food with us and eating lunch was the highlight of the day, besides pay time. I always looked forward to noon.

We got thirty minutes off to eat, always in the shade of the tractor shed. Life was good. My lunch was two slices of cheese, topped with mayonnaise on Sunbeam bread. I also got a bag of chips and a quart of iced tea in a Mason jar with a screw-down metal lid. It was amazing to me that each day the tea was cold and still had lots of ice after several hours in the heat. It was a great meal.

My first year working in tobacco, I was a handler. The job required you to hand the leaves to the stringer who was sitting in a chair. As fast as you could hand him two or three leaves, they were threaded onto the stick. When the sticks were full of leaves, we would hang them up in the tall wood barn. Now that was a job.

We had five rafters inside the barn to climb, and we assembly-lined them up as we worked downward from the top. At first it was scary walking on the rafters that high up, but soon it came naturally. We never had anyone to fall. I recall three of my school friends who worked with me each summer. They were Dennis Bell, John Chauncey, and his sister, Sandra. It was fun to work with them.

My second season, I was a cropper, making four dollars a day. My last season, I made five dollars a day. We would walk down the rows out in the field, cropping the tobacco at just the right time when the leaves started turning yellow. When we got an arm load of leaves, we would place them in a wood sled that was pulled alongside us by a tractor as we cropped the leaves.

Each morning it was cold and wet, and the plants hit us in the face as we started to work. That afternoon we were dirty from the tar of the plants and from being in a dirt field all day. Excitement built when we started down the last row to crop each day. We usually tried singing at that time, but it wasn't a very pleasant sound. The day was over and again we had a pay day.

My third season, the owners had purchased a harvester that was pulled by a tractor, and the stringers were on the harvester with us, four croppers and four stringers. We had to pick leaves at the speed of the tractor and hand them to the stringers as the tobacco leaves flopped in our faces most of the day. It was all right. I was happy making five dollars a day.

I will never forget the day Ms. Nobles' grandson wanted to ride with us. That afternoon he fell off the harvester, it ran over him, and he was pinned under a wheel. This harvester was very heavy, but the other boys and I lifted the machine and were able to get him out from under the wheel. We were only boys and many times later, we tried to pick up the harvester and were never able to do it again.

We took turns carrying the boy a half mile out of the field to the nearest truck, and the men got him to the hospital. He ended up with a broken leg, and we were thankful that his injury wasn't worse.

I'm thankful for the opportunity I had as a boy to work in the tobacco fields. Later, as a parent, I got my son a job working in tobacco one summer. What was good enough for the dad was good enough for the son. I think he may disagree with me on the joys of working in the field.

I doubt my grandchildren will ever work in tobacco. Those days are over. I was talking with a tobacco farmer recently, and he said they grew six hundred acres per year here in South Georgia on his farm. They no longer have croppers or stringers. A machine does it all now. I need to find time to go and check that bad boy out.

Times change.

KETCHUP

Working after high school and on Saturdays at Suwannee Swifty grocery store in Homerville was a good job most of the time. It was a job inside, out of the heat, the hours were good, and it paid $10 per week. During the week we stocked the shelves with food as it was delivered to the store, so I was a stock boy. On Saturday I bagged groceries and changed into a bag boy.

Years back in Homerville, we almost had a ketchup shortage, and it was my fault. As we were stocking the shelves, I grabbed a case of ketchup to put on display. All was going well until I dropped the case of ketchup in glass bottles on the floor. It was not a pleasant sight or experience. Glass and ketchup were everywhere.

After I told Mr. Mac what I had done, he told me to clean it up and to mop the floor when I was finished. It was not an easy job. About an hour later, the ketchup and glass were gone, and the floor was spotless. I felt bad, but life goes on.

It is now Saturday evening, my favorite part of the week. After the last customer left, we would clean up and get paid. My take home pay that week was 47 cents; no, not dollars, cents. That was $10 minus 28 cents for Social Security withholding and minus $9.25 for a case of ketchup.

At the time, this experience was not good in many ways. Forty-seven cents take home pay wouldn't buy much, even in those days. However, I did learn a few big lessons in life that week. Number one, never drop a case of ketchup in glass bottles. Number two, when someone gives you a job, do your best and show respect. It was only right that I had to pay for the loss. I still like ketchup.

DOUGHNUTS

When I was in the ninth grade, I worked at the Suwannee Swifty grocery store in Homerville on Saturdays. I like those old stores compared to the ones of today. We had three aisles and a meat counter in the back of the store. Mr. Mac was our manager. He was firm and didn't believe in breaks or goofing off. He said we should always find something to do before he had to ask us to do a task.

Each Saturday morning around 7 a.m., the two bread suppliers would bring in fresh bread to sell that day, Merita and Sunbeam. I didn't have anything against Sunbeam bread, but the Merita route man would bring us a dozen fresh doughnuts each Saturday. They were awesome!

The Sunbeam man never gave us anything, but then he shouldn't have had to. I'm not sure how it happened, but the Merita man asked us to help sell more of his bread one Saturday. We bag boys asked him if we helped sell all of his bread, would he bring us another box of doughnuts that evening? He said yes without any hesitation.

To accomplish the feat of selling all the Merita bread, we had to have an in-store battle between the two bread companies. It was simple, really. When a customer came to check out, and they had Sunbeam bread, we just asked them if we could swap it out with Merita. Most people didn't really care, and they let us make the change. When the Merita man came in that evening, he got a big smile on his face. His bread rack was empty. He went back to his truck and brought us in another box of doughnuts. Life was good. Well, it was almost good.

Soon after the Merita man left, the Sunbeam man came in. He walked through the front of the store and saw that all the Merita bread was gone and all his bread was still there. He looked like he was going to cry. I felt like scum. I *was* scum. We didn't think about his job, his family, or being fair to him. We sold him out and used our friends to do it. It was not right. We were bag boys who wanted an extra box of doughnuts. I think that's called greed. The idea was great at 7 a.m., but awful at 7 p.m. I vowed to myself never to do that again, to help one person succeed at the expense of another person losing.

I didn't even eat one of those darn evening doughnuts.

JACK'S RIDING MOWER

I will never forget my former boss, Jack Godfrey, and his wild lawn mower ride. It happened in Jesup, Georgia many years back, so I'll pass the joy (or pain) of it on to you. I always visualize the story as a movie, so hold on for the ride.

At the time, Jack was a recent graduate of Georgia Tech and was working one of his first jobs in a paper mill. He was very proud of his recently acquired new home, his yard, and an adjoining two acres of land with a pond in the back. Sometimes ponds were dug so the dirt could be used to build a road, and we used to call those borrow pits. Over the years, our South Georgia drawl made the name sound like "bar pit".

According to Jack, one of the happiest days of his life was when he was able to buy a brand new riding mower from the Western Auto. As a young college graduate with a new family and a lot of financial obligations, Jack decided to purchase his new mower on credit: a little down payment and twenty-four easy monthly installments. Life was good.

Occasionally Jack had to work the graveyard shift at the mill, and on those occasions, he got home as the sun was coming up. On one of those days, he decided he had enough energy left to cut his grass with his shiny new mower. Hey, he didn't have to push. He'd ride in comfort.

The ride that morning turned out to be a little too comfortable. The morning was still cool and the hum of the motor and the slow motion of the mower were like a lullaby. Pretty soon, Jack was asleep on the mower. Yes, I said asleep. I'm not sure if you have ever tried this at home, but it's not recommended.

Jack said he awoke just after he drove the mower into his twenty feet deep pond. When he first hit the water, he thought, *Darn, I have twenty-four payments to make. I've got to save this mower!* He threw it into reverse, but by then the mower was floating...sort of.

As the mower began to sink, Jack held on, trying to stand up in the pond. The mower was too heavy and eventually, he had to make the smart decision. Yes, even a Georgia Tech graduate can sometimes figure out when to let go. It wasn't an easy thing to do, but it was the smart thing.

The story did end well. Later that week, Jack swallowed his pride and had a wrecker come haul his mower out of the pond. When everything dried out, it cranked right up, so making the twenty-four payments was tolerable, and life was, once again, good.

HOGZILLA

I have a so-so friend who helps at my antique shop on Saturdays. Gene Potts is set in his ways, loves to talk more than any other human being I know, and has an opinion about everything.

Gene likes to tell shoppers that he's my number one man. I always smile when he says that, and sometimes I agree and other times I disagree. He says he has to be a good worker, because I have fired him seven times and rehired him each time. He says, "Jimmy can't get along without me, so I always come back. He needs me."

Here's an example of why I have fired Gene seven times. Two families from Berrien County were in my shop one day. They were together and were very friendly people, enjoying themselves digging through my antiques. One of the families had a very pretty high-school-aged daughter. As we were chatting, I said, "Ya'll certainly have a pretty daughter. I bet she is Miss Berrien County. They smiled and said no, but they were pleased with my comment.

Then, Gene has to get into the conversation. He says that the girl could easily be a queen in a local community festival, such as a Dogwood Festival or Honey Festival. Gene was doing okay so far. Next, he asked if Berrien County had any of those type events, and the people said no, the county didn't sponsor a festival.

Not content to let it go, Gene says, "Wasn't Berrien County where Hogzilla was killed?" One of the men said that it was. "Then Berrien County needs to have a Hogzilla Day," Gene adds. "Your girl could be the Hogzilla Queen." If you've never heard of Hogzilla, it was a super large hog killed back in 2004, weighing around 800 pounds and stretching about eight feet in length.

Gene's attempt at a compliment didn't go over well. The two families looked like stunned fish gasping for air, but no words came out of their mouths. What do you say to the suggestion that your daughter could be a hog queen? In a few minutes, the shoppers were gone. We have never seen them again. I felt horrible as they walked away, and I was at a loss for words, except for Gene: "You're fired!"

I don't think any young lady would like to wear the crown of Miss Hogzilla.

What a day.

STATESBORO BLUES

When I was in my last year of college at Georgia Southern, my roommate Joe Posey and I worked at a gas station on the weekends. We went in on Fridays and worked from 6 p.m. to 11 p.m. On Saturdays our schedule was 7a.m. until 11 p.m., and on Sunday, we worked from 9 a.m. to 10 p.m. We made about a dollar per hour, working thirty-four hours per week.

Mr. Brown, the manager, would turn the station over to us on Fridays and before he left, he always took an inventory. On Monday, he counted everything again, and if the money came up short, he would deduct the difference from our pay checks. We were always close, maybe a dollar or so off once in a while. He never told us if we were over on cash; only the shorts were recorded.

When we got off work each day, we usually went straight home and to bed. It seemed like the mornings came early and we didn't get much sleep. With this job, we thought we had nothing but long hours, work, and very little rest. Then came the weekend I will never forget.

Right before we closed one Friday, a friend dropped by and asked us to come by his apartment when we got off. We went and didn't get home until about 2 a.m. Saturday morning. We had to get up at six Saturday morning to get to work on time at 7 a.m.

We did okay for only getting three hours sleep the night before. By closing time we were beat, but before we closed some other friends invited us to their place after work. I don't understand how we had the energy to go, but somehow we found it. The result was that we got back to our apartment for another 2 a.m. bedtime.

Now it's Sunday, and we report to work at 9 a.m., but only in body. Naturally, we had a plan. One would work the pumps, the other one would nap, and then we'd switch off. It worked until late in the day when I woke up from my nap time to find Joe next to me, sound asleep. We had both been asleep for more than an hour, so we had no idea who had been to the station or what they might have taken. When we left that day, it was straight home and to bed.

Pay day rolls around. When we go to get our checks, Mr. Brown greets us with a smile. "I'm not sure what happened this past weekend, but the numbers were not good." Turns out we were short close to 90 dollars. We weren't surprised, but hated to hear what he said next.

"You boys let 90 dollars get away, so I'm not going to be able to pay you this week. As a matter of fact, I'm going to have to hold out 10 dollars from both of your checks next week." Darn!

We continued working for a few more weeks and then decided the number of hours we had to put in weren't worth what we were taking home. We gave notice to quit, and we came up with a new plan: walk to classes and eat less.

Lesson learned: If you do not sleep, you cannot work. If you do work, you can't sleep there.

About Tin Cans and a Baseball Glove

At the time of this story, our family lived in Hazlehurst, Georgia in a middle class neighborhood on the edge of town. My son, Jay, was about nine years old at the time. I learned so much from him as he and I grew up together.

One day Jay informed me that he needed a new baseball glove. We had the money to get him one, but a father raising children needs to teach them about working to get what you want in life. That's the way I had been raised, and I wanted Jay to understand that you didn't just go pick up stuff at the store. It costs us something to get anything of value.

So, Dad had a plan. Jay and I would ride our bikes each afternoon after his school and my work, and we would pick up cans to redeem. When we sold enough cans to come up with the money needed, we would go buy the glove of his choice. He was on board with my plan.

The first day we rode and picked up a few dollars worth of cans. We gave the motorists a few days to litter the roads again, and we picked up cans in the same area. We got about the same number of cans the second time out, which is a whole other story about why people throw junk out their car windows.

Other stuff got in the way, so we took a break and went back at it the first of the next week. This time out, as we go down the road, we see someone on a bike riding toward us. He was an old guy, worn-out and tired-looking. He was picking up cans, too, so we spoke to him and let him get on down the road from where we were. We then turned around and headed home, figuring that he had cleaned the road in the direction we had been going.

That evening, Jay says, "Dad, I don't really want that ball glove anymore." He looked real serious, so I asked him why. "I've been thinking," he said, "and I believe that man we saw today needs the cans worse than I need a glove."

Wow! Jay and I took the cans we had picked up so far and littered them out here and there along the road, hoping the old man would be back the next day. That's the only time in my life that I've been proud to be a litterbug.

Dad learned a big lesson that day. Some people may say that Jay just didn't want to work anymore, and the old man was just a good excuse to quit. No, at age nine, my boy had (and he still has) a heart of gold. He did the right thing. I was on a mission to teach him to earn things in life. He was on a mission to teach me how to love other people. Life is good.

JUST A THOUGHT

In my mid-forties I decided to go back to graduate school to get a Masters Degree in management. Most of my business career was spent in manufacturing companies, working at all different levels, and I enjoyed what I did at each level.

I was still working, so when I started back to school, I enrolled in Central Michigan University's off campus Masters Program. I went to class every other weekend for two years to get the degree in management, and for the most part, I enjoyed the experience.

One professor in particular taught me some lessons that stuck with me over the years and helped me become a better manager. He was an older gentleman who had lots of experience teaching and working with various companies. He was on the staff at Auburn University, but taught a class on good management practices for Central Michigan.

This professor had compiled a list of companies, dividing them into two categories: the most successful companies over a certain period of time, and the companies that had failed during that same time period. He had researched these companies to see what the differences were between them.

It turned out that they all had products that were good, but the ones that had succeeded had the following priorities for their management group's attention: 1) Customers 2) Employees 3) Management 4) Stockholders.

The professor said companies that catered to stockholders and management first had not survived for the long haul. The companies that were successful in his study did all they could to keep the customers happy. You work for your customer first and foremost. Then, smart management provides a caring atmosphere for their employees with above average pay and benefits.

Once a company takes care of its customers and employees, they will take care of the company. It makes sense, doesn't it? Why would a smart customer buy from anyone else when you are catering to his every request? Why would employees do anything to hurt a company that cares about them and pays them better with more benefits than they can get elsewhere?

I am a believer of this business approach, having lived it and worked it for most of my life. I'm not sure how many who read this story will be starting a company or will be on a management team, but if you are one of those people, the truth has been spoken here for your success. Just a thought of mine.

GOOD JOB, BAD JOB

I remember something a former boss of mine, Don Maynor, said years ago when he was retiring from the company where we worked. He didn't really want to retire, but the company's approach to business was changing, and Don didn't like the direction it was going.

Don said, "You need to support who you work for or go to work for someone you can support." That statement stuck with me from that day forward. At the time I was fairly happy with my job and the company, but after Don left we had many changes that I didn't like. The over-all problem was that decisions were being made in a corporate office that was remote from the manufacturing plant, with little input from those of us who were in the plant every day.

I had to take part in some of those changes, and that fact still bothers me. For example, our Plant Manager was told directly from corporate that ten of our supervisors would not get a raise that year. We were to take the amount they would ordinarily get and give it to the highest performers.

The Plant Manager, three other managers, and I had to pick the ten people that would not get raises. I hated to be part of this decision-making group, but I had to be. We made the decisions and then told the supervisors who weren't getting a raise some version of why they were being left out. Of the ten, all of them had worked for the company for twenty years or longer and were important members of the team we had built.

I felt like the positive morale we managers had worked hard to build would start to go downhill, and you could see it happen, starting the day we had to tell them that they wouldn't be getting a raise that year.

Guess what? The next year the Plant Manager was told, directly from the corporate office, that he needed to reduce the number of supervisors by six. Darn, I'm again part of the management group to decide who to fire. We did what we were told to do.

At that time the plant was very profitable and in great shape. In my opinion, this decision didn't have to be made. I think it was just greed on the part of the higher-ups.

I was the one who had to tell the six supervisors they had lost their jobs. One was a former neighbor of mine. Another man was within six months of retirement. What we were made to do was not right, and I found myself part of a system that I no longer respected.

Many times at night, I thought about what Don Maynor had said on his retirement day about supporting who you worked for. I had done that even though I hated being a part of it. As a manager I had made many wrong decisions, so I felt like what was happening was some kind of payback.

After having to do things I was not proud of, I asked for a transfer to another job and was granted that request. A few years later more reductions were made in our workforce, and I volunteered to be one to leave. It was my turn. At the time, it was a very difficult decision. Looking back, it was for sure the best option for me. I'm still saddened by the way the company treated its loyal employees and the part I was forced to play.

My feeling was and still is that any good employer will treat supervisors and employees with respect and will do the best they can to reward them for a job done well.

One of my good friends and another past boss, Gary Foster, states it this way: The first rule of leadership is to trust employees. The second rule is to give them reason to trust you.

Looking back over my work life, I was blessed with some great bosses. Good people make good managers, and these men were the best, each in their own special way: Jack Godfrey, Duke Campbell, Gene Sammons, Don Maynor, Ken Dirks, Cephus Turner, and Gary Foster. Good role models and good people.

COTTON PICKER

I've had several hard jobs in my life, but from what I've heard, I was blessed since I never had to pick cotton. Some cotton pickers have told me stories about that work in the old days, and I enjoy hearing stories that relate to life as we knew it back in the 1950s and 1960s. Come to think of it, there probably aren't many people still alive who picked cotton by hand, so this is a vintage story.

My friend, Jack Godfrey, said that when he was a boy growing up in Baxley, Georgia, he rode by the Western Auto on his bike one day and saw a dream come true in the window. It was an official-sized basketball, and he just had to have it. Jack goes home and tells his Dad about the ball, hoping maybe he will buy it for him.

"You really want that ball, son?" his Dad asks.

"Oh, yes sir." It's looking good. Maybe his Dad is going to say, "Well, go get in the car, and we'll go down to the store, and I'll buy that baby for you."

Instead, his Dad says, "Mr. Sellers's cotton crop is ready to pick, so I'll get him to hire you, and you can earn the money to buy that ball."

Darn, but okay. Got to have that basketball, Jack thinks. Early the next morning, with paper-bagged lunch in hand, he is at the Sellers farm, ready to pick cotton. From early that morning to late in the evening, Jack picked cotton. The rows looked long and the day got hot, but he did his best. He observed that some pickers were better than others and most of them moved faster down the rows than he did, but he kept at it.

At the end of the back-breaking day, Mr. Sellers weighed each bag of cotton and immediately paid the workers in cash. Woohoo! When the farmer weighed Jack's bag, he had to throw out a few rocks, and the boy made a little over a dollar. All day: one dollar and change. At this rate, Jack figured, he had about seven more days of extremely hard labor to get that coveted basketball. That evening, his Dad asked him how his day in the cotton field went.

"Daddy, I really like football more than I do basketball, and I already have a good football."

"So," his Dad said, "You're ready to get out of the cotton-picking business?"

"Yes, sir."

"Okay, but you need to call Mr. Sellers and tell him that you don't plan to be back."

Jack said he was glad to make that call. I'm glad I missed that line of work, too, but many families didn't have a choice. It was one of many jobs they had to do to support themselves. I'm certain that members of those families who took on the hard work of their day have more character, better manners, and more pride than most people today. Hard work is the best formula for success.

Thanks, Jack, for a good cotton-picking story.

SOME GOOD PEOPLE
IN MY LIFE

Ms. Tye

One of the best things that happened in my educational experience was to have Ms. Tye as my ninth grade English teacher. She had a way about her that made me want to learn and work at doing better. She was kind and gentle, and not once did she ever raise her voice or paddle anyone. She controlled her class with respect and gentleness.

One day she asked us to write a one page short story. I turned my story in, and the next day she had graded all of them and returned them to us. She would take time to go over each student's story and talk with us about them.

It was my turn, and when I got mine back, it had two grades on it. One grade was a D and the other was an A. She went on to explain that the D was for grammar and spelling mistakes. I could tell it was not good with all the marks in red and words circled.

Then, she said, "Jimmy, this is the best story I have ever read. That's the reason you got an A. While you are in my class, we're going to work on improvements in spelling and grammar." I was thinking, best of luck with that, because I knew I was bad at those skills.

Then she added this statement: "Which college do you want to attend when you are out of high school?" Does she know I failed the fifth grade, I'm thinking. Can anyone who failed the fifth grade go to college? Ms. Tye was the first person among my family or teachers who hinted that I might be college material. I finished her English class with an A and later took typing classes under her for two years. Yes, she was the one person who gave me a new vision on education and life.

In the early nineties I was influential in starting a continuing educational program in Jeff Davis County to help adults learn to read and to get a General Educational Diploma (GED). We were not part of the local school system, but just a group who wanted to help others help themselves.

We raised the funds to pay for a teacher and to rent a classroom. In a few years, this program was recognized state wide. I didn't know that someone had nominated me as Georgia's Continuing Education Volunteer of the year. I had a big surprise when I was picked for the award.

When I was presented the award in Atlanta, I told the audience that I could only credit the honor to one teacher in my life. It was Ms. Tye. Her nod of encouragement to a ninth grade student years earlier was all that was needed to motivate a young fellow with no dreams in life and no plan for success. We all need to pass the torch of encouragement forward every opportunity we have.

Thanks, Ms. Tye.

MS. MOYER

It was the last six weeks of my senior year in high school when Ms. Moyer made a believer out of me. She was my English teacher and was very smart. She pushed all her students to do the best we could. At the time I had already been accepted to college and had a solid B average in her class. Life was good.

Back in 1968 we had no air conditioning in our classrooms. The teachers had fans for themselves, and that was it. In South Georgia, May and June are always hot. One day, during this time, I was hot and tired of school in general and homework in particular, especially English. I calculated that with my first five six-week averages, I did not need to do much to finish with a passing grade of 70. According to my math, all I needed was a 45 final grade to pass for the year. So, I quit. I went to class, and that was all I did. I didn't do homework, no studying, and life was good.

It didn't take Ms. Moyer long to see what was going on, and she asked me what I thought I was doing. I informed her of the plan, and she didn't respond. We now have a week left in school and finals are coming up. She called me up to her desk to go over my grades. When the evaluation was over, I did have the 45 grade average. I was right. Then she said I needed a seventy on the final exam to graduate. I had miscalculated big time, and the final test would tip the boat up or down.

"Jimmy, I sure hope you make 70 on the final so you will graduate." So did I. "I hope you don't make any less than 70, because I will not give you even one point. If you have a 69, you will fail. Good luck, and if you don't pass the final, maybe you can go to summer school." Darn, not looking good. Now I had to study every evening on everything I had been ignoring in English. It looked impossible.

The big day is now here: senior English final. I took the test and then went over and over my answers. Usually I was the first student to turn in a test, but now I was almost the last. When I handed her the test, Ms. Moyer asked me how I thought I'd done.

"I'm not sure," I answered. "I think it'll be close."

"I hope you get the 70, because I'd hate to see you fail this class. Let's go ahead and grade your paper to see how you did." Gee, thanks.

As Ms. Moyer graded, I tried to keep up with the deductions. As she was finishing, my calculations said I was out about 30 points. She went through the test twice to make absolutely sure she got it right, and the final score was... 70! She congratulated me and wished me well.

I learned a big lesson about not settling for less than what we can do and about the difference one point can make in life.

Dolphus Smith

Recently, I was talking with my first cousin, Ronnie Smith, and the conversation brought back memories of staying in his parents' home when I was a child. Ronnie was one of six children from Uncle Dolphus and Aunt Ruby's clan. Ronnie, his brother Butch, and I were close to the same age, so we did lots of things together growing up. No stories to report there.

I spent many nights at Uncle Dolphus' house, and I will always have fond memories of those times. For one thing, Aunt Ruby's cooking was great. When she cooked, it was a table full of food. The second thing I remember is how Uncle Dolphus would bless the food at each meal.

He was an ordained minister who preached throughout South Georgia during his lifetime. He also worked with the county road department full time. He was known as the wiregrass country preacher. If you don't know what wiregrass is, then you're not familiar with the ole days in South Georgia. I know, but I'm not going to tell.

Getting back to meal time, before we could eat, Uncle Dolphus would start blessing the food. He would pull his chair away from the table, so he could get on his knees. We never knew when he would end, so we kids would nibble from the plates while he prayed. Many times when he finished, we would be through eating and would head out to the yard to play.

He had to know we had been eating, since most of the fried chicken and French fries would be gone, but he never let on. That was a sign of a good man.

Yes, Uncle Dolphus was a firm believer in prayer. The three of us boys would play in the yard till dark and then come back inside for a bath, Bible reading time, and more prayer. Soon after that, it was bedtime.

We all slept in the same bedroom, parents and kids. Each night before Uncle Dolphus came to bed, guess what: More prayer time on his knees. Many nights we would fall asleep while he was praying. I'm certain I stayed in one of the most prayed-over homes in Homerville, maybe in all of Georgia.

Praying was no fade with Uncle Dolphus. I can say without a doubt that he prayed his whole life and loved his time with the Lord. He and Aunt Ruby were special, God-fearing, kind, and loving people.

I know we all get lost at times, and some of us more than others. As I reflect on my childhood memories, what a blessing it was to have seen and to have experienced the lifestyle of my Uncle. If he were still alive, he would tell us prayer is the answer, even if we don't know the question. Any time and any place is a great time to pull out the chair and get on our knees.

Two Great Neighbors

When I was growing up in Homerville, our house was between the Smiths and the Stricklands. Uncle Haskell Smith and Uncle J.M. Strickland were two men who were blessings to my life. Neither of them was really related to me, but that's how close I felt to them, that I would think of them as my uncles.

My dad died when I was young, and these two men stepped in and helped look after me. I want to share some of the highlights of what they did for me and the things I learned from them as I was growing up.

Uncle Haskell had one of the biggest hearts of any person I have ever known. He worked hard, but took time for family activities, including hunting and fishing with us boys. I enjoyed many trips with him and his family to air shows, fairs, and to church. I can't count the number of nights I spent at the Smith home or the number of peanut butter sandwiches they fed me.

I will never forget the day I killed my first buck deer with Uncle Haskell and his son Danny Ray. It was the first deer Danny Ray and I had ever seen while hunting. When the deer came out of the woods, he bounced on the dirt swamp road about ten yards in front of me. Danny Ray was about ten yards behind me. I'm thankful that Danny Ray didn't shoot and take down the deer and me.

Yes, Uncle Haskell Smith was a great man to have as a neighbor and friend. I have many good memories growing up thanks to him.

From Uncle J.M. Strickland, I learned how to work and to sell items from a store. He owned Homerville Supply Company. It was the place to buy furniture, sporting goods, home materials, and electrical and plumbing supplies. The store was open all week except Sunday, and Uncle J.M.'s family members helped him in the store, including his wife, Aunt Agnes, his brother Frank, and his two sons, Wink and Mike. Danny Ray and I were Saturday helpers.

Uncle J.M. knew how to make money in retail sales. He was good at buying items at a price that would make a profit. I watched and learned from him for many years, and except for two weeks vacation and Sundays, he was at the store every day. I learned that when you were caught up with customers or with stocking the shelves, it was sweeping or dusting time.

As Uncle J.M. worked the cash register, he always had time to visit with each shopper to make them feel at home. Their problems were his problems and that wasn't just to make money. He really cared about people.

Haskell Smith and J.M. Strickland were great men, and they were great influences on my life. Life is good.

HEROES

A small town is the best place in the world for kids to grow up. I really feel sorry for children who grow up in our major cities in America. In my opinion, we need a government program of relocation.

One thing I adored about growing up in a small town was the character of the men. They knew you by name, knew your family situation, and in my case, looked after a lost kid like me. I learned a lot from the men in Homerville, and I want to share a tad about two of them.

I worked off and on with Mr. C.W. Pittard from the sixth grade through high school. I cut the grass at his home and worked on his egg farm, loading the truck and making deliveries.

Mr. Pittard was in his late seventies when I started working for him. He loved football, and he once showed me a picture of him and his classmates on the Georgia Tech football team. He played for Coach John Heisman! Yes, the one the Heisman Trophy is named for. I loved that picture and always wanted a copy to hang on my wall. Mr. Pittard was proud of those days, and I wish I could remember all the stories he told me.

Mr. Pittard was the most even-tempered man I've ever been around. Here's a story to illustrate what I'm talking about. One day I was delivering eggs into town in his 1960 black Ford Falcon pick-up, and on the way back to the farm, I rear-ended another truck. It damaged the front end of the Falcon pretty good. It was drivable, but darn I didn't want to take it back to him. I didn't have a choice, though.

As soon as I got back to the farm, I confessed. He looked sad, and so was I. Then, in one sentence (He was not long on words), Mr. Pittard said not to worry about the truck, and we needed to get back to work. He said he needed me to take another load of eggs to town. He loaded up one case of eggs, and it dawned on me that he didn't need those eggs taken to town. He just wanted me to know that he still trusted me. That is forgiveness.

My other hero growing up in Homerville was Mr. Pittard's son-in-law, Dr. Allen I. Robbins. This man was number one in my book. My mom worked for him as a nurse, and he was my football coach when I played in the kid's league that was called midget football. His son, Charlie, and I were friends from birth, and his daughter, Jan, was like a sister to me.

Dr. Robbins was a small town family doctor and that was exactly what he wanted to be. When we were sick any day at any time, we just went to his clinic or his home, and he took care of us. He never turned anyone down for treatment, and he never seemed worried about payment.

I will never forget the day Dr. Robbins died. I was staying with relatives while my mom was in the hospital in Valdosta. We were watching on a black and white TV as Neil Armstrong walked on the moon. That was the news of the century.

Later that day we heard that Dr. Robbins had died of a heart attack. It was like losing a father to me, and it was a shock to all the people of Clinch County, because he was only in his late forties. Dr. Robbins was a special kind of guy, who only comes along once in a century.

I was super blessed to have been around these two great men and their spouses. Dr. Robbins had two older children, Bubba and Bebe. They were kind, like their father and mother, and they were easy to get along with. Kindness and character overflowed from the Pittards and the Robbins families. I was blessed by their influence on my life, as were so many other Clinch County folks.

GOOD INFLUENCES

Homerville, Georgia was a great place to grow up. One of my few regrets in life is that I didn't go back there to live and raise my family. As we become adults, we have to go with the flow of our lives. We do what we think is best at the time, and Homerville was not part of the flow of my life when I was starting a family.

All the same, I like to tell you about the men who influenced my life for the good when I was growing up in Homerville, so here's a story about two more of the great men who mean a lot to me, Dr. Mack Greer and Reverend Paul Barrett.

My mom worked as a nurse, and Dr. Greer was one of the doctors who employed her. He was a very likable man, and he helped look after me. When I was in high school, if I needed to see him for any medical reason, he would say, "Come on in the back door of my office, and I'll take care of you." He never charged my mother a penny for treating me.

What I liked most about Dr. Greer was that he liked to play chess. When he found out that I wanted to learn, he invited me to his home to play. I think he and I were the only two people in town who liked chess, and we played games many nights.

Of course, it was hard for a high school kid to beat a doctor in chess, but occasionally I did, and when that happened, he was in awe. I taught myself to play chess, and I am now teaching our oldest grandchild. I hope I have time left to teach them all.

The other thing I recall about Dr. Greer was that he always made sure I had Christmas gifts under the tree. I still recall the shoes, shotgun shells, and many other items he gave me. Yes, he was a blessing.

Reverend Paul Barrett was the father of my classmate, John Barrett, and he was the man, as far as I was concerned. Hours and hours I would spend with him and his family. Brother Barrett loved to fish in the Okefenokee Swamp, and he must have taken me with him hundreds of times. We enjoyed catching the fish and then cooking them with all the trimmings like hush puppies and French fries on some island in the swamp. Now that is life.

Brother Barrett was influential in my decision to join the church, and he helped me make a change for the better in my life. The relationship with him was very important, and it still impacts my life. As an adult, I have made many right and wrong decisions. However, because of Rev. Barrett's teaching and time spent with me, I do know there is a greater power than people. God is full of forgiveness and grace. We just have to take time to ask God to help us and to get back on track where we left off.

I'm sure these two great men of Homerville, Georgia helped many other kids like me over the years. What good influences they were on my life, and I'll never forget them.

THANKS, FSP

My uncle, J.H. Raulerson was my favorite storyteller in our family, and I loved to spend time with him. One of the last stories he told me was about when he was working for the Georgia State Patrol (GSP). It's a story about men and women doing their jobs and the dangers they faced each day they reported to work.

The surprising part of this story is that I'm thanking the Florida State Patrol (FSP) and not the GSP. As the story unfolds, you'll understand. I'm sorry that I don't have the name of the trooper from Florida who is a major part of this story.

Uncle J.H. was working in his patrol car near the state line between Georgia and Florida. He received a call from the FSP asking permission to come into Georgia on a high speed chase of a dangerous fugitive. J. H. gave permission and joined in the pursuit as the man blew past him.

The outlaw enters Echols County and makes a quick turn down a dirt road. My uncle lived in Echols and knew all the roads, so he radioed the Florida trooper to stop and both of them would block the dead end road that the fugitive had taken.

"That road is surrounded with cypress bays and swamp land," he told the trooper, "so that old boy is going to be coming back out here sooner or later."

Uncle J.H. carried a rifle in the trunk of his patrol car. He retrieved it and leaned up against a pine tree waiting for the man to come back. The Florida trooper drew his pistol, and they both waited.

The two troopers hear the car coming a short while later. The driver slams on brakes just before he would have hit their cars. As the fugitive stops my uncle realizes that he has forgotten to load his rifle. The man raises his pistol and aims it at Uncle J.H. A shot rings out, and my uncle thought he had just been hit.

Thank goodness, the Florida trooper fired first. His shot shattered the fugitive's windshield and with glass in his eyes, the man couldn't see to fire his gun. My uncle and the Florida trooper arrested him. This story reminds me of what our law enforcement people are up against every day. It was bad in the old days, and I think it's even worse today.

BEST STORYTELLER OF ALL

Anyone familiar with Jeff Davis County, Georgia will tell you that Cephus Turner was the best storyteller ever. He had some good company with men like Jack Godfrey and Burtis Taylor running very close behind him. I loved to be with these guys when the tales started and didn't want to leave once they got going.

Cephus was my hunting pal, boss, and friend. He did stretch the friendship at times, when I went to work and folks would meet me in the hall with grins on their faces. That was a sign that Cephus had beat me to work, and the tales were alive and well.

When Cephus told a tale, it started off close to the truth, but didn't stay there long. Some stories he told on me actually were true. I'll give you three he told on me. Two of them are true, and one of them isn't. You'll have to figure out the false one; I'll never tell.

Tale one: We were neighbors, and Cephus spent the day raking his yard. He had ten large piles of leaves and left them to go to town. Being a good neighbor, I went over and set each pile on fire, so his yard would look spotless when he returned. I love the smell of burning leaves in the winter.

He returns and gets out of his truck as I'm standing there watching the last of the piles burn down. He starts crying. He is so sad, because he had planned to burn the piles that evening, sit in a yard chair, and watch the fires while he listened to his truck radio. He finally forgave me and laughed the pain away. That Monday at work, he badmouthed me about what I had done. Everyone had a good laugh at my expense.

Tale two: The next Monday morning story on me was that Cephus had come up on me in the woods, and my truck was stuck deep in the mud. He claimed that he asked me why all four of my tires were flat. I supposedly told him that I'd heard if you ever got stuck, let all the air out of your tires and you'll have more traction to drive out of the mud.

He said he asked me if it worked, and I said, "I'm still in the mud, aren't I?" He told the crowd at work that he pulled my truck out and went to town to get an air tank to fill the tires back up. Everyone had another good laugh at my expense.

Tale three: One morning on a deer hunting trip, Cephus said he noticed a baby food jar in my gear. "What's the jar for," he supposedly asked me. He said I told him that I had read when you are hunting and have to take a urine break, that good hunters would have a jar with them.

If you just did it from the deer stand to the ground, the deer would easily smell your urine and would stay far away. If you went in a jar, you would kill more deer. That part of the story made sense.

But, Cephus told everybody at work that I had told him that my jar was too small. When I filled it up, I had to pour it on the ground and then refill the jar. This story really hurt, but Cephus had a great time telling it, and it did get lots of laughs.

I miss my buddy. I bet he is now on the storytelling circuit in Heaven.

CALLAHAN, FLORIDA

I always have good thoughts when I think of Callahan, Florida, and it's all because of one man I met there. I can't recall his name, but I guess I'll never forget his kindness and what he did for me.

My Mom had moved to Jacksonville, Florida for a short time soon after I graduated from high school. It was my first summer out of school, and I had worked hard to buy my first car, a 1960 Chevrolet. Over the past seven or eight years, the car had been used hard, so I only paid $300 for it. I was pretty happy at first, but after about six months, the car was almost a goner. Later, I ended up selling if for $60, if that gives you any idea of how bad off it was.

Anyway, one weekend I was giving a female friend of mine a ride to Jacksonville to see her parents. She was spending some time in Homerville with an aunt and uncle and had decided to go home for a couple of days.

You can take short cuts through the South Georgia pine woods to get from Homerville, Georgia to Jacksonville, Florida, and that route eventually takes you through Callahan. When you take the short cut, you come into Callahan a back way that leads to a ninety degree turn and several railroad tracks just outside of town.

The trip from Homerville to Jacksonville on Friday night went fine, so I took the girl to her parents and then went to spend time with my Mom. On Sunday I picked up my friend, and about dark, we went back through Callahan, headed to Homerville.

When we came to the bad curve outside Callahan, I overshot it, and we rattled across several railroad tracks, but we didn't make it all the way across. We were hung up, and when we got out to see what the problem was, we found three busted tires and rims. I couldn't get my old car to budge an inch.

A man and a woman drove by, and when they stopped, I asked them to get a policeman to come out. I was nervous about being stuck on the railroad tracks. In a few minutes a policeman did show up, and he was helpful, his only concern being to help me get off the tracks. He called a wrecker service and stayed with us until the car was towed off the tracks.

Now we're at the wrecker station in Callahan on a Sunday evening, and the owner is talking about getting us a room to spend the night. I explained to him that the girl and I weren't married and that I had to be at work at 7 a.m. on Monday morning, so we couldn't spend the night.

"How much money do you have?" the man asked. I like a straightforward businessman. Show me how much you have, and we can go from there. I had $18. "I guess I need to find you some rims and tires, so you young folks can get to Homerville, then."

The man had new rims and tires on my car, and we were ready to go by 10 p.m. He accepted $18 for towing me and for selling me three new tires and rims. I don't guess I have to tell you that he didn't make any money and gave up a Sunday evening of rest to help out two teenagers.

In addition to his wrecker service, he had a full service gas station, so for years after that night, I would make it a point to need gas when I went through Callahan. I'd always stop and visit with that nice man and thank him again for what he did. I'm sure that anyone from Callahan who reads this story will know who I'm writing about. Men like that are always well known by the people around them.

But, our night was not over. We left Callahan at ten, and I made sure to slow down at the tracks this time. A few miles up the road, and the rain started up, and I do mean a downpour. I reached to turn the wipers on, and darn, they didn't work. For the next two hours, I drove with my head out the window. It's one of those things you don't enjoy at the time, but you know a video of it would be pretty funny.

I drove slowly, we made it to Homerville about 1 a.m., and I dropped my friend off at her aunt's house. I managed to get a few hours sleep that night, but before I dozed off, I thought of my friend in Callahan. He was a life saver who helped a young man get home and to work on time, without much thought for his own comfort or profit.

I lay there in bed, thinking: I hope I'm that kind of man one day.

SCARS

A scar in life is generally damaged skin tissue that has healed following an injury or wound, leaving a mark in the process. We can also have scars as a result of emotional or personal situations that are more painful than a physical injury.

As I have become older, I look upon scars as signs of courage and wisdom gained. They can actually become encouragement to us. Let me tell you about some of my scars.

One Sunday afternoon, when I was a boy, our family went on a walk. On the way home I started racing to see who could get home first. I took a shortcut and ran right into a barbed wire fence. The wire missed my right eye by about a quarter of an inch and left a deep cut just under it.

When my Dad heard me yelling, he scooped me up and took me to Dr. Robbins. That's one of the advantages of living in a small town. You can see a doctor whenever you need to. Dad held me down while Doctor Robbins stitched the wound shut.

I still have a small scar under that eye, but things could have been worse. I actually find joy when I see that scar today, because it reminds me of the love of other people for me. My Dad showed that he cared when I remember how concerned he was as he carried me to the doctor. My problem wasn't thought of as an interruption to Dr. Robbins' day. He just wanted to help me.

I have another scar near my chin that can be seen, and it reminds me of a painful day I'll never forget. I got that one from Dr. Robbins' son, Charlie. One day at football practice, I grabbed Charlie in an arm lock from behind. When he broke out of my grasp, I took his right elbow to my chin and my teeth went right through the chin. Another doctor in our little town, Dr. Greer, sewed me up this time.

I find much joy now in this scar. You see, Charlie was one of my best friends of all time. He was smart, easy-going, even-tempered, and he would give you the shirt off his back. Together, we fished, camped, shot guns, played sports, spent the night at each other's houses, and had long talks about life. Folks from Homerville who knew Charlie as I did will tell you that he was one of the greatest and most-liked personalities to ever grow up in Clinch County. My friend Charlie died accidently when he had a seizure, fell into some water, and drowned. We were about forty years old at the time. His unexpected death was painful to his family and all of his friends. I felt like I lost a brother that day.

As I occasionally glance at the scar he put on my chin, all the memories of the good times we had together come back to me. When I see that scar, it brings joy to think that Charlie left a physical mark on my life.

As our wounds in life turn into scars, it seems to me that we have a choice to make. We can resent the circumstances and the people that caused the scars, and we can become bitter, or we can find a way to grow from the pain and eventually find joy when we look at our scars.

Let us find peace and victory in our scars.

Life is good.

FRIENDS

In many of my short stories I have referenced my two neighborhood buddies. Danny Ray lived across the street from our home, and Wink lived right behind our house. I cannot recall a day when I didn't know these two friends.

Recently Wink and I attended the funeral service for Danny Ray, and I decided to write another story about him and the fun times we had many years back. All I could think about was the Christmas catalog, and the two of us playing church under the pecan tree in Danny Ray's yard, with only his mom in attendance.

Danny Ray and I shared the duties of the church. He would preach one day, and I would sing, then we would change roles the next day. His Mom enjoyed our church a lot, and she was our sole, faithful attendee. Oh, how I wish I had a video of those church days. On second thought, maybe not.

At Christmas time Danny Ray was a sport. While his Mom and Dad worked, he would unwrap his gifts, and we would play with them until it got close to the time for them to come home. Then, he would carefully put them back in the wrappers and everything looked untouched.

He and I really had fun with the Sears and Roebuck Christmas catalog. This was back when kids had imaginations, and you have to be over fifty to relate to what I'm saying. When the catalog showed up in the mail, Danny Ray and I took turns picking out the toys we wanted on Christmas day. One day, he got to pick one from the right hand page, and I had to choose one from the left page.

The next day we swapped, and I got one from the right page and he had to pick from the left. Then we made believe we had those toys, and we played without having to worry about remembering to wrap everything back.

At my antique store, I recently had a customer who grew up next to Roy Rogers' ranch in California. He shared many stories of growing up next to my cowboy idol, but he had nothing on me, growing up next to Danny Ray and Wink. Thanks for the memories, guys.

LIFE IS GOOD

SAD BOY

As I have shared my short stories on Facebook, I have been blessed with positive comments from many of you and feel blessed to have had the opportunity to share them. Most of my stories have started with a memory, and it was easy to see and feel the story and stay on track. Those stories had a beginning and an end, and they flowed well.

I haven't felt a flow or order to this next story. As I have attempted to write it, my thoughts have bounced around, slippery and hard to grasp. I think the reason for those feelings is that in order to write it, I've had to deal with past pain that I was trying to avoid. I force myself to write this story, because I hope it turns out to be an encouragement to the reader. Maybe the best I can do is to write it the way I told it to my wife June a few years back.

My parents divorced in 1960 when I was eleven years old. Both of them moved to Valdosta from my little safe world of Homerville. My Mom had a nice home where we lived, and my Dad lived in a small apartment upstairs in some building. His health and his drinking problem were both bad.

I missed my Homerville friends beyond measure. I was in a new school, which I didn't like, and I spent most of my free time by myself. I really didn't care about much of anything, except being with my Dad. I got to stay with him every other weekend. We didn't really do anything special, but I was with him and that was enough for me. The only problem then was that it hurt me bad to see the pain he was in and to know that there was nothing an eleven-year-old could do to help him.

On a Friday night in April on one of the weekends when I wasn't with him, we got a call that he'd had a heart attack and died. The call came late at night, and my sister Sonja and I were both awakened by the ringing phone. We overheard the conversation between my mother and whoever was on the other end of the line. The last time I had seen my dad was the previous Sunday when I was at his apartment. Sonja and I were heartbroken.

When I told my wife about this time in my life, I related the events of that last Sunday with my dad. I knew he was in a lot of pain that day, and my feelings of helplessness overwhelmed me. I went out on the porch to the apartment building, sat down on the steps, and cried.

Across the street was one of the largest churches in Valdosta. While I sat on the steps, crying, I saw families driving up to go to church. As they got out of their cars, they were talking and laughing and enjoying life. I knew it was a church and that these people were there to worship God, but in my simple mind, I was just hoping someone would come across the street to ask me what was wrong and to help my dad.

God may be there in that building, I remember thinking, but its hell over here where I am. That's the way I remember my last visit with my dad. I felt alone and useless, and I hurt for my dad.

When I told June this story, she said, "Jimmy, I have something to tell you. Please listen to me. Even though no one came from across the street to help you or your dad that day, there was someone sitting on the porch with you.

"God was there, and he felt your pain. He knew He was going to be your new father. God is the father of the fatherless. Whatever you've needed from that day forward, He has provided for you. That day wasn't easy for you, but He was there that day, and He's been with you every day since. He hasn't always given you what you thought you wanted, but He's met every need in a timely way and in the way that's best for you."

June was right. I have been blessed. God was there on that day, and though I'm not worthy of His love and have made a few thousand mistakes in my life, God has always had my back.

He has given me a love for children that has become one of the great passions of my life. I make sure that I speak to kids, hug them, give them little gifts, and say encouraging things to them. We never know what a child is going through, and a smile can go a long way to heal some hurt they're experiencing.

I have already told you some stories about special men that God put in my life after the death of my father, and I have some more of those stories for you. Those men were my fathers, bringing me out of bad situations, offering encouragement along the way, and helping me see dreams that I might bring to life. My Father God inspired them to help me.

I have been on missionary trips to different places in the world, and it's good to go out from where we live to serve other people. But, our biggest mission field should be right where we live. Often, when I drive by a church, I ask myself if the people who worship God there know the people who live right across the street. If they saw a little boy sitting on the front steps, crying, would they go ask him what they could do to dry his tears? We should.

Life is good.

Fifth Grade, Second Time

When we moved to Valdosta, I was eleven years old and in the fifth grade. My teacher, Ms. Atkinson, was an older, loving teacher who tried to help me. She would stay after school, talking to me about my father's death and trying to encourage me. It was hard to get through to me, but she tried, and she was a good influence in my life.

Many years later, I was working at a gas station on the weekends while I was in college. Guess who drove up for gas: Ms. Atkinson and her husband.

"You probably don't remember me," I said, "but I was in your fifth grade class in Valdosta, and I want to thank you for trying to help me back then." She seemed happy to see me, and we chatted for a while. I think she was totally surprised that of all her students, I was one of them who made it to college.

At the end of my fifth grade school term, my mom had a discussion with Ms. Atkinson about what would be best for me in the next school term. My teacher suggested that I repeat the grade in another school in Valdosta the next year. So, that became the plan, and it turned out to be a good one.

The next school year rolled around, and there I was in a new school, with a new teacher, and new friends. I did keep two good friends from that first year. Jerry Brooks and Rhett Dawson were my hang-around friends after school and my spend-the-night buddies.

My new teacher was Ms. Logan. Compared to the year before, I was now in the top of my class. I was so smart that it really wasn't fair to the other students, but this was my second chance. I became active in little league baseball, midget football, and the Boys Club. Life was good...again.

After the second year in Valdosta, we moved back to Homerville. I came back a top notch student that next year and stayed that way for the rest of my school years. Repeating a grade or two is not all that bad. I know our educational leaders nowadays do not want students to get left behind. Based on my experience, I'd say they are wrong.

T AND G

I've studied about personality types in my working career, and I remember that one classification labeled personalities type A and B. The type A personality was achievement oriented. Type B was easy-going. Now, I'm introducing two new personality types: T and G. T stands for tightwad and G is for generous.

I think we all cross the line at times from one type to the other, tightwad one day and generous the next, but I want to encourage all of us to become a G and stay one.

We had a speaker at our church one Sunday named Gary Atkins. He was a member who had some thoughts to share about Christians and generosity, so the Preacher turned him loose. Gary did an outstanding job and quoted scripture to make his point. That's when the creation of the T and G personalities started in my mind.

Gary said that if you ask a waitress the worst day of the week to work, she will probably say Sunday. They say that Christians complain more and tip less than any other customers.

The general rule of thumb on tipping is to leave fifteen percent, so Gary suggested leaving at least twenty percent. It's our chance to show someone we don't know very well that we care for them and appreciate them serving us.

Also, Gary said the worst meal for a waitress to work is breakfast. The cost of the meal is lower than the other meals, and most people think a dollar is plenty to tip at breakfast. His advice is not to worry about the percent of what the meal cost, but to give generously. Try leaving a five dollar tip at breakfast to see how it makes you feel and to see how much you think you're helping a waitress feel good about life in general.

Gary went on to say that if we Christians can't give good tips, we'd do better just to stay home and eat. You can be a T type personality at home by not tipping your wife. Tipping is part of the cost of eating out, but more importantly it gives us a chance to show who we are: G, not T.

Even when the food at a restaurant is bad, the waitress still deserves a tip. She's serving you, not making the food. If you don't like the food, just don't go back to that restaurant.

My wife won't let me complain when the service or the food is bad. She says we never know what a waitress is going through at home, so we should not make her day worse. She might have to deal with sickness, financial problems, abuse, or a hundred other negative things that we aren't dealing with. It made sense to me, so I am now a non-complainer.

In the end, Gary Atkins made a difference in the way I think about generosity. I still have a ways to go, but I'm moving from a T to a G more every day. Here is an illustration of why you don't want to be a T personality.

I had a type T friend who was on a business trip. After one of the meals, he picked up the tab and left the tip. As he and the other men left the restaurant, the waitress called out to ask him to wait for her in the parking lot. When she caught up with him, she gave him his tip back.

She said, "Sir, this is no tip, and I think you must need this money more than I do." Wow, how do you think he felt with the other men witnessing this act?

Here is why you want to be a G personality. Another friend of mine was on a trip to Alabama. While he and some other men were eating, he saw a bus load of young people coming into the restaurant. They came in and some of them sat at a table next to him, so he started talking with them.

The group was a choir of black young people who were on their way to do a concert at a church in the area. My friend was so impressed by their good manners and friendliness that he picked up the tab for the whole choir. My friend was a true G personality.

Another friend of mine and his wife lost their home in a fire. A week later he received a letter from an old friend in another town. Inside the letter was a check for five thousand dollars.

Are you a T or a G? If you've been blessed and can afford it, move in the G direction. A great opportunity awaits you.

My Friend Ronnie and His Baseball Cards

When I was a kid, back in the 1960s, I had a lot of fun going to the store and buying a few packs of baseball trading cards. I had a good collection, and sometimes I would luck up on a Mickey Mantle, Sandy Koufax, or Willie Mays card. I loved to trade cards with my friends, and I think that's when I developed the habit of trading antiques and bigger things with friends.

I still recall tossing those cards in the trash the day I was packing up to go to college. I guess I was thinking that I was too grown-up for such childish things then. Dumb. That was so dumb.

I didn't realize how dumb until I ran into one of my card-trading buddies years later. I asked him if he still had his collection, and he said no, that he'd sold them. I asked him how he did, and he informed me that he made enough to pay for one of his son's college education. Wow! That was good and bad news wrapped up in one conversation – good for him and bad for me.

Ronnie's story of baseball cards is different from any that I have ever heard. Ronnie was a general contractor in Hazlehurst, Georgia, and we became friends, because we liked to go treasure hunting together on weekends, mostly at yard sales.

One day we were looking through some of our recent finds at his home, and he showed me boxes and boxes of baseball cards. They were newer cards, so they didn't have much value, but as we were looking at them, he said he needed to tell me something.

Ronnie said that baseball cards were special to him. Years earlier he had started drinking, and alcohol soon got control of him. I knew that he'd had a problem at one time, but I never saw any signs of it when we were together.

His drinking eventually got so bad that he couldn't even work. One evening he went to town to buy some liquor, but he didn't have enough money, so with what little money he did have, he bought some baseball cards. Laughing, Ronnie said that purchase made no sense, because he wanted a drink, not cards.

When he went back home, he spent the whole night looking through his cards. He would place cards in stacks by teams. Then, he would rearrange them by the states the players were born in. Next he would stack them by the age of the players. He said he must have come up with a hundred different ways to arrange those cards.

He made his first day without a drink that way. In the next few days he went from dying for a drink and overcoming the shakes to gaining sobriety card by card. Many weeks after buying more and more cards, he was a sober, working man once again. I loved his story.

Ronnie stayed sober the rest of his life. He died from cancer, but before his death, he called me to come see him. He had made a wood frame for me and framed a silver dollar for a friendship gift and for good luck. It still hangs in my office and when I glance at it, I'm reminded of Ronnie and what a box of baseball cards helped him accomplish. Life is good.

What'd You Call Me?

At times I think we're living in the craziest, most unfriendly days since creation. People are looking for ways to find fault, even when no fault is intended or has occurred. Some people just live for turmoil. This story is all about words. I once heard that the meaning of words is not in the word, but how the hearer interprets the words; so true.

Many years ago, the company I worked for sent me to the Chicago area to attend a class in team-building. There were thirty of us in the class, and we all worked for the same company. Most of the people were from the mid-western United States, primarily the Chicago and Houston areas. Overall, it was a good group of folks to be around for a week.

One important note: I was the only one in the class from South Georgia. I brought along with me the Georgia-type personality and all the trimmings. The purpose of the class was to enrich team-building skills, and to take them back to implement them in the work place.

The first morning we were out climbing walls and doing other activities that required teamwork. The instructors had divided us up into four teams of about eight people each. Of course, I wanted to win, and in one of the first events I used the word, girls, to cheerlead my team members along. Mind you, I was only referring to the girls on my team.

My exact comment was, "Come on, girls! We can do this."

The instructor came over to me a tad later with a request. She said the word, girl, had offended some of my team members. What? Offended them? I explained to her that it's a common word we use in South Georgia, with no offense intended. After our little chat, I told her I would not use the word again… g word?

My commitment lasted until the next event. I love to win, and in the heat of the moment, I used the g word again! I got to have another conversation with the instructor.

The next night the class was having dinner together in a social atmosphere. The instructor was moving around, talking with the various team members. When she stopped with my group, I was ready for her. I told her I had a bad dream about this class, so she wanted to know what it was about. Of course, I had made the dream up, but I had a point to make.

Before I told her the dream, I informed her that in South Georgia, the word girl is not offensive. Actually, even old ladies and most females I know have never been offended when referred to them as girls. But, I did take her comment seriously the day before, and I was trying to avoid using the word.

Now to the dream: I was a ladies basketball coach. I had eight ladies or females on my team. I wasn't really sure what they should be called. In South Georgia we call them a girl's basketball team. I am so confused in my dream.

The whole group around the table was now into the dream and where it was going. I told the instructor that I had five females on the court playing against the other team. A few minutes into the game, I said, "Come on, girls! We can do better." One of the players walked up to me and quit on the spot. I asked her why, and she said she did not like being called a girl, and she was gone.

A few minutes later, I said, "Come on, ladies. That's not the way we play this game." Guess what? Another one ran over to me and quit. She did not like being called a lady. Darn!

Then, in my dream, I remembered the word I had heard all week in this class, so I decided to use what the instructor had taught me. She was listening close to me now and asked me what happened next.

I told her that the next time the team made a bad play, I said, "Come on, you guys, we can do better than that, and then guess what happened. Two more players came over and quit. I didn't have enough players to continue, so we had to forfeit.

I told the instructor that in South Georgia the word, guys, refers to males, men or boys. In this class it seems to refer to all sexes. It sounds right, seems right, but it's not the right word where I come from.

She thanked me for sharing my dream, and told me that I made a good point. She and I were big buddies the rest of the week. On the last day of class, we were called up to get our completion certificates. I was shocked when the whole class gave this South Georgia Boy a standing ovation. Did I say, boy? Maybe I should have said, guy.

Why are we so hung up on words? As long as we're kind and encouragers, the words won't be too far wrong. Life is good.

DEAD DOG

When I was growing up, my favorite television shows were Bonanza, Roy Rogers, Andy Griffith, The Price is Right, Art Linkletter, and The Ed Sullivan Show.

The Art Linkletter Show's theme was Kids Say the Darndest Things. It came on each weekday in mid-afternoon for thirty minutes. During the show, Art would talk with four kids, most of them in the first or second grade. He had a way of bringing funny stories or comments out of those kids, as no one else could.

My wife June shared this story she had read in a book about Art Linkletter and one of the children from the show. Art would meet with the children the day before they were scheduled to be on the live performance show. He talked with them, so he could get a feeling for their personalities and how they reacted to questions.

One day in the interview process, a particular boy was very outgoing and talkative, but the next day on the show, he clammed up. During the live show, Art asked him if something was bothering him. The boy responded that he was very sad, because he had found his dog dead that morning.

Linkletter said, "I'm certain your dog is in heaven with God now." The boy looked Art in the eyes and said, "What does God want with a dead dog?" Can you imagine the expression on Art's face? What do you say to a question like that?

The moral to this story is to be careful what you say to your children. They're probably one step ahead of you in their thinking. Mr. Linkletter lived to be 97 years old, and he brought a lot of laughter into people's lives in his day by showing us the wisdom of children. It may be a good idea for us older folks to hang around the younger crowd more often. Children produce the fruit of laughter, and that's good for us.

CAT IN A BAG

When I worked in a manufacturing plant in Hazlehurst, Georgia, I loved to go to work on Monday mornings. How often do you hear people say that? I worked in the human resources area, and part of my job was to chat with employees, to start their week off on a positive note. I would ask about how their weekend went and go with the flow of the conversation. During those years, I made lots of friends and listened to lots of stories.

One Monday I saw a group of five people listening to a friend tell a story of his weekend. I got there late, and the whole group was dying laughing. I asked the storyteller to tell me what happened, and here is his story.

It's Saturday morning, and he and his wife are planning a trip to the shopping mall in Waycross. He goes out of the house first and finds a dead cat out in their yard. He puts the cat in a paper bag, puts the bag on the back floorboard of the car, and gets in the car to take the cat to a vacant lot nearby. About that time, his wife comes out ready to go, so he decides just to bury the cat when they get back.

They're now at the mall, and the day is beginning to heat up, so he's rethinking his plan. He decides he'd better set the bagged cat out of the car while they shop, or they'll have one stinking car in a few hours. He puts the bag on top of the car, and as he's walking into the mall, he's thinking, *Wouldn't it be funny if someone stole that bag?* It was just a thought. Who would do that?

As his wife enters the mall, he takes up his customary place on a bench outside to wait on her. He's not into shopping. After about five minutes, he sees a large lady walking across the parking lot toward his car. She wobbles to his car and in one smooth scoop has the bag under her arm.

She continues through the parking lot and finds a bench in front of a drugstore, just down the sidewalk from where my friend is sitting. She couldn't wait any longer to see her prize. She places the bag between her legs, glances around, then peeps into the bag. My friend watches the lady as she hollers and passes out. People gather to help her, and someone calls 911.

In a few minutes help arrives. The EMTs load the still-unconscious lady up in the ambulance, and as they're about to close the doors, someone yells, "Wait, this is her bag." They place the bag carefully on top of her and off they go to the hospital.

My friend sits there on his bench, smiling and wondering how the story ends at the emergency room. I've often wondered that same thing.

MOWER THINKING

When I cut the grass in my yard, I cut in long stretches until I have to go around plants or trees, and then I cut rectangular and square patches. The long stretches are particularly good for thinking.

One day as I was mowing, it occurred to me that in my whole life, I have not cut a yard the same way twice. Have you? I have always tried to figure out the best path to save time, and I always come up with a little bit better way. After all these years, I've finally decided that there probably is no best way. Just do it.

If there was a best way, someone would be selling the concept on an infomercial, or you could call 1-800-yard-pros for a Google Earth map layout.

Another deep thought I had while mowing involved my murder story.

I don't have plans to kill anyone, but what if I did murder someone with or without cause? For the purpose of this story, I will go for "without cause". When I get caught, this is what I would do.

First, I'd plead guilty. I did it. We don't need a trial, so we can save the taxpayers' money.

Next, I'd tell the Judge, "I don't want to be locked up for the rest of my life, so let's save some more money. I'll go with the death penalty, Mr. Judge. I'm a big boy."

At that point, I wondered if there would be anything to look forward to in prison until they could get me executed. (I'm still on my mower, remember. I haven't killed anyone.) Yes, I decide: There will be a last meal. I understand that you get anything you want under those circumstances, so here is my last meal menu.

I would want Paula Deen to prepare the meal, not some random, tattooed, bald-headed cook in the prison system. I'm going with all Southern, home-cooked food like all the women in my family used to dish out, plenty of salt, butter, and fatback. What have I got to lose? They're getting ready to fry me!

Here's the menu: fried chicken, roast beef with plenty of rice, creamed potatoes, potato salad, creamed and boiled corn, fried and boiled okra, butter biscuits and fried cornbread, butter beans, pink Crowder peas, black-eyed peas with snaps, greens, pork chops, rice and stewed tomatoes, sliced tomatoes, green beans with early potatoes, salmon patties, fried and boiled squash, rutabagas, sweet potatoes, sugar-cooked carrots, and deviled eggs.

For dessert, I want pecan pie.

Since I saved the taxpayers the cost of an expensive trial and keeping me up for ten or twenty years while the gears of justice slowly ground away, maybe I could get seconds.

With that thought, my darned mower runs out of gas, and the story ends here. Well, not quite. It's supper time, and I have to choose between Zaxby's or the Dairy Queen. So long, Paula.

Life is good.

ENCOURAGEMENT

We all hear folks say that when they win the lottery, they will do things to make this a better world – right after they buy a new car and a new house and pay off their bills. There's nothing wrong with a little dreaming. I dream, too.

But even if we're close to being poor, and we don't win the lottery, aren't there some things we can do to make the world better?

When the weather is cold, and we're afraid our water pipes might freeze, what do we do? We leave the water dripping just a little. I try to keep that thought in mind each day as I go out into the world to work. I may meet someone whose pipes are close to freezing, either emotionally or financially. I try to listen with my heart to hear someone who needs just one drip of encouragement.

Drips of encouragement can be a smile, a word of appreciation or concern, a tip, a phone call, handshake, hug, a meal, a card, and even a wink and a smile or a simple hello can brighten someone's day.

When the temperature is freezing, a drip of water may keep the pipes from bursting. A drip of kindness, concern, and encouragement can certainly help others in ways we will never understand, but they will.

GOD IS WILLING

An old phrase from years past has popped into my mind, and I cannot seem to get it out. It may be a good sign, such as I have little to think about, or it may be a bad sign that I am forgetting what I need to be thinking about.

"... If God is willing and the creek don't rise." That's the phrase. You can put most any statement in front of the phrase, such as "I'll see you soon if God is willing and the creek don't rise." Some people say, "... if the **Lord** is willing and the creek don't rise" but I won't split hairs.

I also notice that no one uses the word, "doesn't". I guess that would make the English teachers happy, but "don't" sounds better and that's what everyone says. Also, if God is willing, whatever you put it front of the phrase will happen, don't matter what the creek do. God is in charge.

Since I can't seem to get the phrase out of my mind, I put on my research hat and learned a couple of ideas about how the phrase originated. Here you go.

It's said that a farmer promised to help plow a neighbor's field, a neighbor who lived across the river from him. It rained too hard, though, and he couldn't get his mule over to the neighbor's farm. Rain being an act of God and the river's depth dependent on rainfall led to the phrase.

I like the second explanation better. It sounds too good not to be true.

Colonel Benjamin Hawkins (b. 1754 – d. 1816) is credited with the phrase, correctly written as "God willing and the Creek don't rise." Notice the capital C on Creek. The Colonel wrote it in response to a request from President George Washington to return to our nation's capitol, and the reference is to the Creek Indian Nation. If the Creek "rose", Hawkins would have to be present to quell the rebellion.

Now I have found peace with this phrase. Tomorrow, if God is willing and the Creek don't rise, I can get the phrase out of my head. Sorry if you read this story and now you have it implanted in yours. Not really. Deal with it.

MOMMY SAYS

Recently a friend of mine came close to bumping her head on a door. I said, "Be careful. Don't hit your head."

She said, "It wouldn't hurt me, I'm so hard-headed."

I said, "You have a good point."

We had a good laugh, and then she was a little indignant.

"You didn't have to agree with me," she said.

"Well, you claimed being hard-headed, and my mommy used to say, 'If they say it, and it's true, you can agree with them.'" My friend laughed a little, but I knew my boat was in the process of sinking and trouble was on the way.

The reply I got back was: "Well, my mommy said you need to keep your trap shut at times and be nice."

Both our mommies were right. So, which road do I need to go down if a similar event occurs?

I think I'll go with my friend's mommy's thoughts: Keep my mouth shut and be nice.

How about you?

NO WIGGLE ROOM

Growing up in a single parent home, my life was tough in many ways. Anyone who knew my Mom had learned that you did not want to upset the woman and that included me. Rule number one in my teenage life was not to make my Mom mad.

Mom did not give me any wiggle room. She made the rules, and I had darn better do as she said or else. The else wasn't pleasant.

As I started going out some at night on the weekends, she always gave me a time to be home. There was no wiggle room on that deadline. I only tested her on that rule one time. It wasn't actually my fault, but I didn't make it home by 10 p.m. and that was the set time.

It happened this way. I had gone to a classmate's home for a chip, dip, and Coca-Cola party. I had walked to the party, which was about a mile from our house. When the party was over, one of the guys had a car and offered to take me home. Okay.

So, now I'm in my friend's car with four other kids. We go by Clyde's Drive-In café, the common weekend hang-out. Clyde made the best hamburgers and fries in the world, and for 50 cents total, you got a Coke with the food! I had time to spare on the curfew and all is good.

About this time someone said, "We need to go to the Mill Pond. There's going to be a fight." Now, that's high entertainment in a small town. It seems that a guy who had Homerville roots, but didn't live there now, had dated a Homerville boy's girlfriend, so the fight was on.

I knew I ought to go on home, but I couldn't miss a fight. It didn't last long, and the guy from out of town was the loser. He was winning until a brother and a friend of the hometown boy decided he needed a little help. Rule number two in life: Never date another guy's girl if you're from out of town.

The fight didn't last long, but it lasted too long for me as I was about an hour late getting home. I am truly praying as I walk into the house. I'm asking God to make my mother be in the bed. Nothing doing. I see her coming from the kitchen with a chair over her head. She is not saying nice things and doesn't seem all that happy to see me. Thank the Lord, she did put the chair down before she got close enough to use it. She gave me an earful, and then sent me on my way to bed.

That was my first test on wiggle room. I've found out in life that there is not much wiggle room to be had. We have to deal with the rules of other people more often than not, and it's important to know the boss's definition of wiggle room. Don't count on having much.

OUT OF TOWN

When I was a sophomore in high school, a senior girl asked me to go to the Junior-Senior Prom. Her invitation was out of the blue and totally unexpected, so I hemmed and hawed and finally told her that I would let her know the next day.

For the rest of the day and that night, I wrestled with the decision. I didn't have a car. I didn't have any money. I didn't want to get dressed up in a white coat, black pants, and polished shoes. I had no desire to go, but a girl had asked me out, and I didn't want to hurt her feelings. Would the other seniors make fun of her? She couldn't even get a sophomore to go out with her.

It is now the next day. I met her and said, "Thanks for inviting me, but I can't go. I'm going out of town that day." Looking back, I really didn't need that second sentence. I was guilty of stretching the truth. No, I was telling a whopper... a lie.

Now it's a few weeks later, the day of the prom. I'm still squirming, and I decide that I won't be a liar. I get on my bike and head out the Fargo highway. I get to the city limits of Homerville, and I pedal another hundred yards or so past the sign. I'm out of town. On the ride home, I'm thinking about how glad I am that I have a bicycle. That would have been a long walk.

Did you know that the word sophomore comes from two Latin words that, roughly translated, mean "wise fool"? I've heard that, but I've never looked it up. Seems right to me.

PERSPECTIVE

Out at the mushroom farm, one mushroom was complaining to another about their circumstances.

"They're always feeding us a bunch of crap and keeping us in the dark all the time."

I guess life is not always fair, even in the life of a mushroom.

I remember as a kid, all the homes in our neighborhood had slop buckets with lids. After each meal, we would place our leftover food in the bucket. Late each week, a local hog farmer would come and collect the slop bucket food to feed his hogs. Usually, just before he came by, there was an awful smell in our neighborhood.

I used to wonder if those hogs' conversations were a lot like that complaining mushroom's statement.

One hog says to another, "I see Farmer Joe coming with more of that slop for us to eat. It stinks to eat food three or four days old that smells worse than the mud we roll in.

"What a life we have. We eat slop and live in mud."

Then his buddy says, "What difference does it make? We'll be bacon soon."

TIME FLIES

I love living in South Georgia, but no place is perfect, and here is my list of things I could do without: the summer heat, gnats, horseflies, yellow flies, and those nasty house flies. If I had to narrow the list down to what God would let me get rid of, there would be no more gnats or house flies.

Gnats will drive you crazy. They attack in swarms, and they love my eyes, nose, and ears in particular. They reproduce like crazy, and wherever I go outside, they are there. What do they live on until I show up? I dream of the day they would be on the endangered species list.

But then, house flies also drive me batty. They love to buzz around me when I'm trying to nap. They seem to be getting bigger and braver and nastier with each passing year. Some are even brave enough to land on me, and that's where I draw the line. As quickly as I can get to the fly swatter, they are dead. We live in the country, so we have a fly killing once or twice a day.

I have a story about flies that I can't get out of my head. Maybe if I tell it to you, I can have some peace or at least some forgetfulness about it.

A friend of mine took me fishing at his brother-in-law's pond one day after work. In no time we caught a good mess of fish. The brother-in-law shows up at the pond and invites us to eat supper with his family, so we oblige him.

After we pack up our fishing gear, we drive over to the house, and it's a pretty normal country home. Cats, dogs, ducks, and chickens all share the same yard in peace. The aroma of food cooking drifts out into the yard, and it's smelling good.

We walk around to the back yard and only a few yards from the house, the brother-in-law grabs a chicken and wrings its neck before the poor old bird knew what hit her. In a few minutes, he had it gutted, featherless, and ready to cook.

"Supper's almost ready," the man grinned. As his wife added the chicken to the creamed corn, peas, fried okra, rice, and cornbread she was already cooking, my friend, his brother-in-law and I sat at a big country farm table and swapped stories. The company was good, but as we sat talking, I noticed more and more flies gathering.

At first I tried to shrug it off, but the more flies that swarmed, the more it concerned me. The darned things were landing on the food and walking around like they'd been invited, too. Nobody else seemed to notice, but I didn't know how I was going to bring myself to eat this great-smelling meal.

After the blessing, everyone started passing food around, but I had no appetite after watching hundreds of flies slosh through the creamed corn, peas, and rice. I guess I was a tad spoiled, but have you ever thought about where fly feet go all day, especially on a farm? And the little devils weren't even making any effort to leave the food as it was passed around. I had to wave them off. Yuck!

Bingo! I finally came up with a plan to spoon down and get the vegetables off the bottom of each dish and then wolf it down before the flies could fly my way. These were good folks, and I didn't want to be impolite, but it was one of the few times in my life that I turned down seconds.

I came to the conclusion that flies are pesky and nasty, but some people aren't bothered by them. I guess to farm folks, flies are just part of life, and they don't pay much attention to them. Maybe it was just the picky ones who had pie safes and fly swatters.

I wish I had more tolerance of the unpleasant things in life, but it's not in me. When I used to complain about things like flies and gnats, my Mom would tell me that those weren't the things that would kill me. They were just nuisances, and if I would build up a tolerance of them, it would make me a better person. Maybe Mom was right. I was sure blessed that day to be with my friend and his family, enjoying their pond and their hospitality and good food.

Life is good. It would be so much better without... well, you know.

IT-DEPENDS-ON-HOW-
YOU-LOOK-AT-IT DAY

Years back, when our daughter was a student at the University of Georgia, my wife and I went to visit her in the first week of July. When Saturday rolled around, it was the fourth of July, and on the spur of the moment, we decided to spend Independence Day touring the north Georgia mountains.

On the drive north we saw a sign pointing the way to Amicalola State Park. We had heard that the waterfall in the park is the largest in Georgia, so we had to see it. If you've never been there, put it on your bucket list. It was getting close to noon, so we pull into a local market and pick up stuff for a picnic: crackers, a few drinks, and fried chicken. You can't have a picnic without fried chicken, at least not in the south.

So now we are in the state park, and the picnic area is full of folks. We park our car and start walking through the crowd, and there's one concrete table in the back. We set up back there, and as I'm looking around two things dawn on me.

First, everyone else had evidently planned their day. They were loaded up with cookers, grills, ice cream churns, coolers of food and drinks, and watermelons. Music was playing from a half dozen different radios or boom boxes, and they were playing horseshoes and throwing Frisbees.

They had come prepared to enjoy the day. We had our one little bagged meal for three. It was quite a difference.

Second, and I'm just stating a fact, not being racist, the three of us were the only white people in the park. The others were all Indians, not of North American Indian descent, but from abroad. They were speaking a language we didn't understand and having a great, big time. We just thought it was odd that on American Independence Day, we were outnumbered.

We went on with our meal, but the longer we sat there, the more we got the feeling that we were the topic of many of the conversations going on around us. Maybe they all thought it was an odd situation, too. They would glance over at us, talk among themselves, and then have a big laugh.

We finished lunch and were off to see the waterfall. We walked up with a crowd of Indian people, passed others coming down the hill, and met still more at the falls. They would all speak to us, and we said our "hello" and "Pretty-day-isn't-it" back to them. Then they would talk to each other and have another good laugh. We're scratching our heads, wondering what they're talking about.

Along the trail, I asked my wife June what she thought the discussions were about.

June has a good sense of humor, and she said, "I heard one of them speak in English, and he said, 'That's those poor white people from the picnic area who were eating fried chicken out of a bag.'"

I guess we were.

Oh yeah, the third thing that dawned on me that day was how nice everyone was to us, the laughing thing aside. I make it a point now when I'm in a big crowd of white people and there are only two or three people of a different race, to speak to them and to make them feel welcome.

ALL YOU GOT TO DO TO BE HAPPY

Here are my criteria for a good song: I can understand the words, I like the beat of the music, and it has a positive meaning, even if it's a little wacky. One of my favorite songs of all time has all three of these elements. Many of you will never have heard this song, particularly if you're under age 30.

Just the title of "You Can't Roller Skate in a Buffalo Herd" by Roger Miller should tell you that it's a little wacky, but if you've never heard it, pull it up however you do that sort of thing and listen to the words. The song may help you have a better day or even a better life.

The song talks about things that you can't do in life, and each verse ends with the refrain that "you can be happy if you've a mind to". I've found that to be true in my life. How happy I am from day to day depends a lot on my attitude.

Here are some of the things Roger Miller says you can't do:

You can't roller skate in a buffalo herd.

You can't take a shower in a parakeet cage.

You can't swim in a baseball pool.

You can't change film with a kid on your back.

You can't drive around with a tiger in your car.

You can't go fishing in a watermelon patch.

I guess the only one that doesn't fit in today is that one about changing film in a camera with a kid on your back. Maybe we'll have to change that one to "You can't focus your phone camera with a kid on your back."

But, here's how Roger advises us to be happy: "All you gotta do is put your mind to it. Knuckle down, buckle down, DO IT, DO IT, DO IT!"

How's your attitude? Find the song, enjoy it, and learn to be happy.

RANDOM WISDOM

Here are some thoughts I've had that didn't fit into any of my stories, but I thought might be a help to someone reading this book.

A good recipe for happiness is to combine equal parts of laughter and kindness and then to stir it into someone else's life. Share it equally with friends and strangers and don't let an opportunity pass you by.

Dream within your bounds, but always be determined to broaden your bounds through hard work, commitment, and honesty.

If sunset represents the past and sunrise represents the future, let our mistakes set with the sun and let knowledge gained from mistakes be present with the glitter of the new day.

God blesses those who do not bury their talents, but use them daily.

By your own thoughts, you make or mar your life, your universe. As you build yourself within, by the power of thought, your outward life and circumstances shape themselves accordingly.

We should not hurt others with words or hate, but build them up through encouragement.

These random bits of wisdom are a good way to wind up this book. I hope you've had a good time reading about my life in South Georgia, and I pray that you'll agree with me that life is good.

That's most of the experience and wisdom I have to share with you, but keep reading. Over the years, I have met some well-known people who have given me the benefit of what they've learned in life. Now, I want to share their wisdom with you, too. Listen to what they have to teach us all, and don't give up on life getting better for you. Keep on pedaling!

APPENDIX

SPECIAL ADDITIONS TO MY LIFE

MAX CLELAND ON COMMITMENT

Max Cleland was a popular politician in Georgia from the early 1970s to the early 2000s. Among other offices, he was a Georgia state senator, Georgia Secretary of State, the Administrator of Veterans Affairs under President Carter, and a U.S. Senator from Georgia. As a young soldier in 1968, Max Cleland lost both legs and one arm in a grenade explosion in Vietnam. Regardless of that tough circumstance, he has stayed the course he set for himself in life and worked his plan.

I once had the opportunity to spend time with Mr. Cleland, and he shared his view of life with me. His thoughts are very personal and just may help you have a better day. Here's what he had to say about commitment.

"Commitment is belief in yourself and in your goals. It means preparing yourself to achieve and believing you are special. Do not let anyone talk you out of trying to achieve a goal, if you truly believe it is right for you.

"Commitment is also an act of courage from within. You must develop the courage each day to get up and do everything possible to move forward, despite what may have happened yesterday. It can be difficult to achieve something worthwhile, and it's easy to give up. Life is a series of ups and downs, so it's not as easy to accomplish some things in life as some people might think.

"Everyone has their ups and downs, and that's just life. The bottom line is to stay on course, to stay with your plan. Do not give up.

"I consider myself a survivor and just surviving counts for something good. I felt like I had to survive, because I wanted to stay in the game of life. But my goal in life is not mere survival. I want to be the best I can be. I want to get that mountaintop experience and make my life count for something. I want my life to have meaning.

"I think the southern author, William Faulkner, put it best when the received the Nobel Prize for Literature. To paraphrase Mr. Faulkner said, Not only would mankind endure, but also, he would prevail. I believe we all endure a lot, but the key to life is not just to endure, but to prevail and to thrive, and to really have a sense of meaning.

"That is my goal. I may not meet it every day, but I am going to be striving to move forward."

Wow, those are great thoughts from a man who knows what he's talking about.

Jimmy Carter on a Daily Walk

Several years ago I attended church one Sunday in Plains, Georgia, to listen to the former president of our country, Jimmy Carter, teach Sunday School.

Many people consider President Carter the greatest president our country ever had; others do not. I do know being born and reared as a Georgian myself, I look up to President Carter, and I respect him. Maybe it's not so much for what he did as president, as for what he has accomplished throughout his life. When life is over, what we did on our jobs, good or bad, doesn't matter as much as whom we were in our hearts.

President Carter averages speaking at his hometown Baptist Church at least two Sundays each month. Afterwards, he takes time to speak to those who attend his class. The commitment he has made to the Lord vouches for his beliefs, considering his work schedule and other commitments around the United States and the world.

His presentation the morning I was there to hear him was encouraging as he spoke about the commitment we need to make to be Christians on a daily basis. He said, "The Bible tells us to take up our cross daily." Then he rephrased it as follows: "We need to take up our cross daily, not annually."

President Carter went on to say, "We must set a goal and pray daily for strength to do what we believe in and to do what is right, one day at a time. The future will be resolved on its own accord if we stay committed to serving God one day at a time."

What great advice.

BOBBY RICHARDSON
ON PRIORITIES

All baseball fans during the 1960s knew about those great New York Yankee teams. They repeatedly won the American League banner each season and were the favorites to win the World Series for many years.

Even though the Yankees were a great team, they were not my favorite. I was a Los Angeles Dodgers fan. I loved to watch their great players, especially Sandy Koufax, Don Drysdale, and Duke Snider.

The Yankees were a close second to the Dodgers in my heart. The only time I would pull against the Yanks was when they played the Dodgers in a World Series Championship game. I wanted the World Series to go seven games, with the Dodgers winning in the bottom of the ninth inning. When I think of the Yankee's team of the '60s, Yogi Berra, Mickey Mantle, Roger Maris, Whitey Ford, and Bobby Richardson come quickly to mind.

You can imagine how honored I was when Bobby Richardson, the second baseman of the Yankees during that great era, spent the night at my home. He was in my hometown to speak at our church about what Christ meant to him. After the service that night, he went home with us, and I grilled him with questions about the Yankees, his teammates, and the grand slam homer he hit to beat the Pittsburgh Pirates in the 1970 series. We stayed up until after midnight, and I had the time of my life listening to him.

Years have now passed, and I can't remember much about the baseball discussion I had with Bobby Richardson. What I do remember is what he said about following Jesus. You see, we didn't just talk about baseball that night. He wanted to talk about how important it is for a person to put God first in his life, then family.

Bobby told me that some of his teammates used to make fun of him as he walked in the Christian faith during that era of great baseball. However, he kept his faith and followed God's plan for his life. The way he looked at it, baseball was his job. The experience was rewarding, but he said no homer, double play, or game-winning hit ever made him as happy as serving God as a Christian.

That was a great night for me. Life is good.

Bill Curry on Listening

Bill Curry played professional football for the Green Bay Packers and the Baltimore Colts. He started as the center in Super Bowls I, III, and V. Later he was the head football coach at Georgia Tech, Alabama, and Kentucky, and he started the football program at Georgia State University in 2008.

When Coach Curry was at Alabama, we had a personal family friend who worked in his office. I asked the friend to get Bill Curry to give me some personal thoughts he had about living a good life. To my surprise, the coach mailed me what I'm about to share with you. Here's what he said in his letter to me.

"I learned how to listen from my daughter when she was 17 years old. At that time, she quit speaking to me for about six months. There were some personal problems, and we were going through hell together. She has always been her own person, just like her mother, and she had decided that talking to her dad wasn't worth the effort. It was killing me to know she felt that way.

"I went from being terribly offended to getting angry, and then on to trying to take charge of her as her parent. I tried to hammer her, tell her who she could and could not see, and in essence, tried to lock her up. I even had her telephone shut off. I did all the stuff stupid dads do to beautiful daughters.

"The day came when I'd finally had enough, and I sat her down for a talk. 'I love you more than my own life,' I told my daughter. 'I have given you everything I have, but it doesn't seem to be enough. What's wrong?'

"'You tell me you love me,' she said, 'and I know you think you mean it, but I don't feel your love. When I try to talk, you NEVER listen. You only think about what you're going to say next.'

"I almost fell out of my chair, and I wept. She was right.

"But we don't fix those kinds of problems in an instant. It takes effort and time. The next week I was in a staff meeting at the University, and I asked one of our coaches his opinion on a very important matter. Don Lindsey is one of the brightest football coaches I've ever known, and you don't have to wonder what's on his mind. If you ask Don for an opinion, he'll tell you exactly how it is.

"He was giving me his thoughts on this particular subject, and about halfway through a sentence, Don just stopped talking. I noticed it, but we just went on with the meeting, and afterward, I asked Don to join me in my office.

"I said, 'Hey, Don, I asked your opinion and when you got about halfway through your thoughts, you just quit talking. Why would you do that?'

"'Yes, I did,' he said. 'I can tell when you stop listening. When you quit, there's no reason for me to continue to talk, is there?'

"I was 44 years old at the time, and I didn't know how to listen to another human being. How was I going to learn anything if I couldn't listen? How was I going to have a good relationship with my daughter and other family members if I didn't actually listen to what they have to say?

"Since that time, I have made an effort to hear what other people are saying to me. I hope you will, too."

SONNY CARTER – A
SUDDEN DEATH

During the early 1990s I went to Jekyll Island, Georgia to attend the annual Rotary Club Conference. One of the main reasons I attended was that I wanted to hear the keynote speaker, Commander Sonny Carter. He was a medical doctor who had dreamed of becoming a pilot. He accomplished that goal, and in 1989, he flew on the Challenger space shuttle. In addition to those achievements, Commander Carter was an inspiring speaker who was dedicated to God and to his family.

As I traveled to Jekyll that day the weather was perfect, but I heard a report on the radio that dangerous thunderstorms were moving into the area. Sure enough, I encountered one violent storm just on the outskirts of the island. As I neared the convention center, I heard another announcement on the radio that former Texas Senator John Tower and at least twenty other people had been killed in a weather-related airplane crash.

I made it to the conference and was enjoying a fine meal and fellowship with other Rotarians when a man went up to the podium onstage. "I regret to inform you that our keynote speaker, Sonny Carter, was killed in the same airplane crash as Senator Tower."

The laughter and fellowship stopped, as we all looked at each other in silent disbelief. It was a nightmare of emotion. My mind was telling me that Sonny Carter had been killed, but I was thinking how unfair that fate was to him and to his family. He had worked hard and achieved a lot already, but he was still a young man. His children were still young.

He was coming to share his thoughts on living a positive life with strangers, but it was all taken from him suddenly.

I tried to draw some rational conclusion from this tragic event, but it was just senseless. Since I didn't have the opportunity to hear him speak, I wondered what difference his speech may have made in my life and in the lives of the other people there that night. The speech wasn't made, but the significance of that night made a lasting impression on me.

We need to believe in God and in the positive things He can do with our lives when we devote them to Him. We need to believe in ourselves and encourage other people to believe in themselves and what they can accomplish. Our actions speak louder than words, and Sonny Carter spoke loud and clear to me by the way he lived his short life.

ERK RUSSELL ON DOING RIGHT

Erk Russell was a great assistant football coach at the University of Georgia during the Vince Dooley era. He was later the head coach at my alma mater, Georgia Southern.

Coach Russell was a great motivator of young people, and he was well-known in his day for butting heads with his players before a game. I'm talking about literally butting heads when the players had their helmets on. Coach Russell was bald, so you could see the cuts on his head and the blood streaming down his face.

I had the opportunity to work with Coach Russell and Gene Crawford, the Director of the Georgia Southern Foundation, on a few projects, so Erk and I became friends. The many good conversations we had were priceless, and I learned that Coach had two general rules that I think would be helpful to you.

Rule number one was DO RIGHT. Coach expected his players to do right when they were not playing ball. He believed strongly that all young people know right from wrong, and he demanded that his players always make the right choices in life.

He didn't want to waste his time and the team's time with athletes who thought they were entitled to excuses for doing the wrong thing and who were constantly getting into trouble. His players at Georgia and at Georgia Southern soon learned that no matter how big and strong of a player they were, they didn't want to butt heads with Erk Russell. He didn't mind getting bloody.

As adults, we should abide by Coach Russell's rule: DO RIGHT. We all know right from wrong, and we shouldn't waste our precious time looking for excuses to make wrong choices in life. Most of our problems would go away if we would only make up our minds to do the right thing in all circumstances.

Erk Russell's second rule was to be committed to whatever you do. He expected his players to GET AFTER THEIR BUTTS. Average play was not acceptable to Coach. When the ball was in play, he expected his players to go full steam every second. It didn't matter if they were practicing or playing on Saturday, every player was expected to give each play everything he had.

As adults, how many of us go through each day halfheartedly, not really committed to doing our best at whatever we're doing? To run a business or to do anything worthwhile in life, we need to go full steam as opportunities present themselves.

Do right and be committed to what you're doing: that's a great formula for living a full life. Erk Russell was a great guy, and I appreciate him teaching me his two rules for living.

VINCE DOOLEY ON
OVERCOMING ADVERSITY

University of Georgia head football coach, Vince Dooley, was a great friend of a friend of mine named Claude Cook. Mr. Cook and I lived in Hazlehurst, Georgia back in the 1990s, and he was a major supporter of the Georgia Bulldogs. When Mr. Cook went to Athens to a ballgame, he always took a crowd of people with him, and I was blessed to go to a game with him one time. We had a blast!

I would often see Coach Dooley in Hazlehurst with Mr. Cook, and one day I had a chance to talk to the coach. I asked him to share some personal thoughts with me that I could put into a book I hoped to write one day. I told him I wanted the book to encourage people and to help them improve their lives, and I think that persuaded Coach Dooley to send me what you're about to read.

Mr. Claude Cook and Coach Dooley were two special men. They enjoyed helping other people, and I am so thankful that Coach Dooley would make a contribution to this book. Here's what he had to say to you and me about overcoming adversity.

"During the twenty-five years that I coached for the University of Georgia, I went through some difficult times. I don't believe there was ever a more depressing time for me and for our fans than the winter of 1974 when we lost to Auburn, Georgia Tech, and then to the University of Miami in the Tangerine Bowl. We were 6-6 that year, and the end of the season was a disaster.

"'We are going to get Dooley,' a prominent state legislator told my offensive coach, Frank Inman. I was hung in effigy. There had been a time when I could walk down the street of Athens and nobody knew me. After 1974, I could have walked down the street, and some people would probably have crossed to the other side to avoid me. My popularity had reached its nadir.

"Never have I experienced such complaining and bickering. I was enough of a historian to understand that these things can and will happen to anybody in my profession. As a matter of fact, it had just happened to Coach Bryant of Alabama, following back-to-back seasons of 6-5 and 6-5-1. The Tide ran up big scoring totals, but was losing too often. The Alabama people were complaining that the Bear was too old and had lost his touch.

"Our fans were saying that I was too conservative, that I didn't even know my players' names and was stuck up and wouldn't speak to anybody. Realizing that I was misunderstood, I told my good friends that I couldn't change my personality. But the truth of the matter was this: when you don't win enough football games, some fans are going to find something wrong with you and the way you coach, no matter what. It may be your offense or your personality or the way you dress. If you don't turn it around, they will, indeed, get you.

"What people didn't understand was that I was the unhappiest person of all with the situation. No group of dissatisfied alumni could have put more pressure on me than I placed on myself. I was determined to keep my mouth shut and to work until things were resolved. If I couldn't get the job done, they wouldn't have to run me off. If I ever concluded that I couldn't deliver, I would have left on my own.

"You must remember that the early 1970s were changing times. We had campus protests stimulated by the war in Vietnam. Attitudes about life had changed all across the country, even in the conservative South.

With my military background, I was perhaps too rigid. I had to change and adjust to the changing times.

"Over the next several years, I became a better communicator and learned to be more sensitive to what our players were thinking and saying. Still, what takes place on the playing field sums up your abilities as a coach to the fans. If you compare the record of our 1974 team with our 1980 National Championship team, you might determine that I was a better communicator in 1980. But, it wasn't just that I was six years older and wiser. It took effort on my part.

"A head coach's job can get lonely in the tough times. When you win, everybody shares the victories. When you lose, only one person must shoulder the blame. As President John Kennedy said after the Bay of Pigs disaster, 'Victory has a thousand fathers; defeat is an orphan.'

"Never had I been more ready for a new season than in 1975. I had to take the heat for the 1974 season. Only I could shoulder the blame. There was no reason for excuse making, as people in the state were preparing for my demise.

"Pepper Rodgers, who had come back to Georgia Tech, leaving UCLA for his alma mater, was drawing a positive reaction with his wishbone offense. He had gained some concessions from the Tech administration and was building a winning program. After Tech beat us in the mud in Athens, the soothsayers generally agreed that he would win the state's fans back to Georgia Tech, like it had once been with Bobby Dodd.

"Even some of our most loyal supporters, including an athletic board member, were saying that we would never beat Tech again. I couldn't concern myself with the complaints and rumors. It was a matter of working hard and resolving to straighten things out.

"Before we could rebound in 1975, which solved a lot of problems and eliminated all rumors about lack of rapport with players and the like, there was a personal matter of great concern that had to be addressed. Not only was I bothered about the potential consequences if we didn't field a competitive team in 1975, with my contract running out, I wanted to eliminate any distractions so we could do a good job of recruiting.

"My sense of security has never made me worry about contracts personally. I could live with a one year contract like the faculty and everyone else on campus, except for that one issue: recruiting.

"High school players don't want to hear that a college program is in transition from one coach to another. It's not the facts that matter; it's the perception that has weight. The perception in the summer of 1975 was that Vince Dooley was in trouble. There he was in the last year of his contract, and a new coach might be moving in to 755 Milledge Circle toward the end of the year. Those kind of rumors are often just that, rumors and nothing more, but they are unsettling to high school players and their parents.

"I felt that we had demonstrated in ten years that we had developed a sound program that had never embarrassed the University and that there had been enough success and tradition established that it was reasonable for me to ask for a renewal. A new contract would stop all rumors, keep our recruiting on track, and keep our team from having to read in the newspapers that 1975 would be my last year as the Bulldog head coach.

"I went to Dr. Fred C. Davison, the President of UGA, to review my thoughts with him. Fred was a president whose contributions have meant a lot to the University. He always believed strongly in the value of intercollegiate athletics. He loved the bulldogs, and he understood my point of view. He didn't hesitate, and the Board awarded me a new four-year contract in late summer.

"The announcement of the new contract took place the day the "Sky Writers" tour hit town. Writers from newspapers in the Southeastern Conference states toured SEC schools each August, along with the T.V. stations in the area. They arrived in Athens right after the Athletic Board had met, so the University and Dr. Davison received a lot of positive publicity for the stand they had taken.

"Suddenly a lot of cynics and yappers were shut up. We could go about the business of coaching and winning football games, which we did with the "Junkyard Dogs."

"Even though we opened with a loss to Pittsburgh in a game in which we made costly mistakes, it was a happy year for us. Of all the teams I've ever been associated with, that 1975 group was really special. It was a very exciting team that won nine games and was good enough for a trip to the Cotton Bowl. Our success justified Dr. Davison's decision at the only time in my career when there was reasonable opposition mounting against my being head coach. The good thing is that we followed the 1975 season with an even better one in 1976 when we won the SEC Conference title, and the Bulldog faithful formed a sea of red in the French Quarter for our trip to the Sugar Bowl.

"By being able to stay focused on my job during the crisis and by being able to devise a plan of action, I was able not only to survive, but to grow during difficulty. I thank God for giving me the foresight to handle adversity in my life."

?

Printed in the United States
By Bookmasters